The Power of

I AM

Compiled, Edited, Formatted & Layout

By

Shanon Allen

&

David Allen

Books for Enlightening and Illuminating the Mind

First Hardcover Edition, February 2016

ISBN: 978-0-9972801-1-1

Visit Us At **NevilleGoddardBooks.com** for a complete listing of all our books and **1000's of Free Books to Read online and download.**

Published

by

Shanon Allen

Editors Notes:

Our first book 'The Power of I AM' was created as a PDF that we distributed freely to the metaphysical community as our way of saying thank you for all the other books out there in the world, that were shared with me.

This book is a response to the loving feedback we have received since then.

Thank you everyone for your kind comments. May this book bless you many times over.

The beginning of each quote is in **bold** print.

Be sure to look for more books from our "The Power of" Series in the near future.

The world is waking up!

Foreword

I AM is our true power! I AM is known as the lost word! The word itself was never lost, but the meaning was! The intention of this book is to help restore that meaning and help change and transform lives! If we succeed in changing even one life for the better then this book has been a success! We believe and are very aware of the many books out there on metaphysics and the law of attraction but we feel this one is quite different in that it may be what most people are seeking and possibly missing. It is my contention that there is not one single secret to our seemingly complex lives but many.

Being positive, being loving toward all, being and feeling grateful every minute of every day for what life has given us, avoiding negativity and judging or criticizing others or ourselves are all things that will improve and help transform our lives. Being aware of who we are and what our words and thoughts are creating in our circumstances of everyday life gives us an advantage over people that simply aren't aware of this. But we believe this book, The Power of I AM, will bring to the reader a whole other aspect to their lives that didn't exist prior to this book and what that means is, we believe, you may find what was missing and preventing you from discovering a better and brighter world beyond just positive thinking.

Introduction

The Power of I AM is not a book to be read once and put on the shelf. It is not going to transform your life just because you read it. If you are expecting it to reveal some sort of secret that, by just knowing it, will transform your life, more than likely you will get very little out of it and will be extremely disillusioned. As I have personally discovered in my own studies of metaphysics, it is not what is contained in a book that will enlighten or illumine me, but what I apply to my life. If there is no application of the laws or revelations contained within this book, then you will have nothing more than a conversation piece. Only those who apply what is contained herein can hope to benefit from its contents. Knowledge alone, while interesting and entertaining, doesn't have the power to change or enrich your life. It is only through the application of knowledge or any law that we can hope to benefit from it. Ten people may read the same book and get ten different results, and it has less to do with the book than it does with the people reading it.

One person may read a book and, without any personal experience, come to a conclusion and deny that it contains any truth. This does not make it so, nor does it confirm what the book claims. Such a reader will not understand what the person who has read it ten times and applied the principles for a year or five years, or just chooses to live life as such, will understand. By following the principles within this book, as with any metaphysical book, *you alone* hold the power to transform, enrich, enlighten and illumine your life, beyond measure. Quite a courageous claim? It is true with most metaphysical books. It solely depends on the reader how much will be garnered from any book.

As someone who has come to appreciate what metaphysics offers to anyone who is sincerely seeking truth, it is with this in mind that this book was chosen for publication. If a reader were to tell me he or she received nothing from reading it I would have to question if the principles contained herein had in fact been applied and practiced. I say "question", because there is no way of knowing if the reader is being honest with us, or themselves. Although "The Power of I AM" as a book is just now being revealed to the world, in the form of a compilation from some of the more insightful teachers of the last century, I believe that all those who read it, now have a chance to see what each and every human being has had an opportunity to realize, before them, through other sources. That is: I AM is who we are, I AM is consciousness, I AM is Love, I AM is a gift to mankind, and I AM is the power that we all possess. If you understand this and apply it, you will discover a new world, in which you can and do live. Once you learn The Power of I AM you will begin to become more and more conscious of what you add to *your* I AM, for what you add to your I AM with feeling will embody itself in your world. Rediscover the meaning of I AM, that has been lost to the world.

Shanon & David Allen

Acknowledgments

I would like to express my gratitude to Andy Morsicato with whom I had many great discussions in 'the garage', about metaphysics, that went on for hours. I appreciated those talks we had and the influence they had on me. The encouragement and enthusiasm that I gathered from those discussions along with the memories, I will cherish forever. I feel very fortunate to have had someone who could discuss the things we did at the depth we did.

I dedicate this book to our daughter Stephanie. We love you!

A very special shout out to all the 'friends' I have met online who have been a part of my journey. There are a lot of good people in this world and I have met many of you and hope to meet many more.

Awaken to the Power

of "I AM"

Table of Contents

The Power of "I AM"

There is only one Master

and this Master is God, the I AM within themselves. "I AM
the Lord thy God who led thee out of the land of darkness;
out of the house of bondage". I AM . . your awareness, is
Lord and Master and besides your awareness there is neither
Lord nor Master. You are Master of all that you will ever be
aware of being. You know that you are, do you not? Knowing
that you are is the Lord and Master of that which you know
that you are. You could be completely isolated by man from
that which you are conscious of being; yet you would, in
spite of all human barriers, effortlessly draw to yourself all
that you were conscious of being.

———————～——————

Your awareness . . I AM . . is the master magician who
conjures all things by being that which he would conjure.
This Lord and Master that you are can and does make all
that you are conscious of being appear in your world.

You rise to a higher level of consciousness by taking your attention away from your present limitations and placing it upon that which you desire to be. Do not attempt this in day dreaming or wishful thinking, but in a positive manner.

Claim yourself to be the thing desired. I AM That; no sacrifice, no diet, no human tricks. All that is asked of you is to accept your desire. If you dare claim it, you will express it.

———————～———————

I AM is that reality to which, whatever happens, we must turn for an explanation of the phenomena of life. It is I AM's concept of itself that determines the form and scenery of its existence. Everything depends upon its attitude towards itself; that which it will not affirm as true of itself cannot awaken in its world. That is, your concept of yourself, such as "I AM strong", "I AM secure", "I AM loved", determines the world in which you live.

The Power of "I AM"

"I AM" is the fact of existence, and to know that gives you all power. When you have to go and tackle the "Egyptians" and your heart turns to water within you, and you say to yourself, "I cannot do this," "I am not adequate," "There is no way," then remember your true identity and say to the "Egyptians," "I AM hath sent me," and the road will open and you will surmount your difficulties. Before man can transform his world, he must first lay this foundation or understanding. "I AM the Lord and there is none else".

———————— ⌢〜 ————————

Man must know that his awareness of being is God. Until this is firmly established so that no suggestion or argument of others can shake him, he will find himself returning to the slavery of his former belief. "If ye believe not that I AM He, ye shall die in your sins". Unless man discovers that his consciousness is the cause of every expression of his life, he will continue seeking the cause of his confusion in the world of effects, and so shall die in his fruitless search.

The Power of "I AM"

Whatever you affix to the "I AM" and believe, you become. The "I AM" in you is God, and there is none other. "I AM" or Life, Awareness, Pure Being, Existence, or the Real Self of you is God. It is the Only Cause. It is the Only Power making anything in the world. Honor It; live with the feeling, "I AM Christ," all day long. Christ means the Anointed One, the Awakened One, the Illumined One. Feel you are this Anointed One; continue to live in that mental atmosphere; then you will draw out the Christ (Wisdom, Power, and Intelligence of God) within you, and your whole world will be transformed by that Inner Light shining in your mind. Every time you feel, "I AM the Christ"; "I AM illumined"; "I AM inspired"; you are praying and qualifying your consciousness with the thing you are praying about, and with the thoughts you are thinking.

———————⟨∼⟩———————

I came that ye might have Life and that ye might have it more abundantly . . I AM the truth, the LIFE, etc. . . "come unto ME" . . blending with this permanent identity will finally defeat the "last enemy" . . and then shall we enter into a plane of manifestation and be freed from the coming and going of this lovely truth.

16

The Power of "I AM"

It is the greatest Affirmation the New Emancipation puts on our tongue. I AM Love directed to my chosen end by thought. The stanza which we sing, "God is Love," comes as the fulfilling of the Law. There is no longer Law for Man but Man for Law. As Sabbath and State are for Man, so Law is now for Man, and Man becomes the Law unto himself, even as God is Law unto his Universe. I AM Law! Can you climb thus high? I AM Law! Hence forth in my freedom Nature obeys me for, I AM Law. And, I AM Law, because I AM Love, for Love is the fulfilling of the Law. As soon as I recognize that I AM Love, then I become in the universe lawless, and becoming Law I live above all Law. In this connection do you recall Emerson's most wondrous lines, "Into the fifth himself he flings, and Conscious Law is King of Kings."

———————~———————

There is but one Truth, one Life, one Intelligence, one Self, one I AM, one Presence, and I AM This. I do not speak with mind. I do not create thoughts. I speak Truth. I speak the Word. I AM the fulfillment of that which I AM.

The Power of "I AM"

As long as you believe in a God apart from yourself, you will continue to transfer the power of your expression to your conceptions, forgetting that you are the conceiver. Do you believe that the "I AM" is able to do this? Then claim ME (yourself) to be that which you want to see poured out. Claim yourself to be that which you want to be and that you shall be. Not because of masters will I give it unto you, but, because you have recognized ME (yourself) to be that, I will give it unto you for I AM all things to all. Your belief in masters is a confession of your slavery. Only slaves have masters. Change your conception of yourself and you will, without the aid of masters or anyone else, automatically transform your world to conform to your changed conception of yourself.

--------⌒--------

We limit our prosperity by the way we identify ourselves. This self identification can be subtle such as: "I AM only...." Be aware of what you tie your "I AM" to. This is a powerful tool of calling the creative process into flow.

The Power of "I AM"

There are not two I AM'S, but one I AM. Whatever, therefore, I can conceive the Great Universal Life Principle to be, that I AM. Let us try fully to realize what this means. Can you conceive the Great Originating and Sustaining Life Principle of the whole universe as poor, weak, sordid, miserable, jealous, angry, anxious, uncertain, or in any other way limited? We know that this is impossible. Then because the I AM is one it is equally untrue of ourselves. Learn first to distinguish the true self that you are from the mental and physical processes which it throws forth as the instruments of its expression, and then learn that this self controls these instruments, and not vice versa. As we advance in this knowledge we know ourselves to be unlimited, and that, in the miniature world, whose center we are, we ourselves are the very same overflowing of joyous livingness that the Great Life Spirit is in the Great All. The I AM is One.

If a man tries to achieve what he wants through external means, it will forever elude him. He is a thief and a robber in the sense that he is robbing himself of the joy of manifesting his ideal, by refusing to claim and feel its reality mentally. He must have the mental equivalent first; then its manifestation follows. Our own mind or consciousness . . I AM . . is the door to all expression.

19

The Power of "I AM"

All I ask is that you who read these lessons shall try the effect upon the subconscious mind of vigorous, positive, living words. Even though you are in the midst of poverty, sickness and sorrow, affirm the opposite. Say with all the earnestness you can muster: I AM Rich, I AM Well, I AM Happy. Say it again and again, though all things conspire to give the lie to your words. If you do this faithfully, just as sure as you live the words you thus utter will fall into the subconscious mind and become there a power to work for good in all your conditions.

***

I AM. What is I AM? It is your true being. It is your real nature, your real self and nobody else, because no one else can say I AM for you. Only you can say I AM. That is your real identity, the Presence of God in you, the Indwelling Christ. That is you, and whatever you attach to I AM with conviction, that you are and that you have.

The Power of "I AM"

Jesus of Nazareth, who scattered the evil with his eye, is asleep in the imagination of every man, and out of his own imagination must man awaken him by subjectively affirming "I AM Jesus" Then and only then will he see Jesus, for man can only see what is awake in himself.

The Kabbalists tell us of "the lost word," the word of power which mankind has lost. To him who discovers this word all things are possible. Is this mirific word really lost? Yes, and No. It is the open secret of the universe, and the Bible gives us the key to it. It tells us, "The Word is nigh thee, even in thy mouth and in thy heart." It is the most familiar of all words, the word which in our heart we realize as the center of our conscious being, and which is in our mouth a hundred times a day. It is the word "I AM." Because I AM what I AM, I may be what I will to be. My individuality is one of the modes in which the Infinite expresses itself, and therefore I AM myself that very power which I find to be the innermost within of all things.

To me, **thus realizing** the great unity of all Spirit, the infinite is not the indefinite, for I see it to be the infinite of Myself. It is the very same I AM That I AM; and this not by any act of uncertain favor, but by the law of polarity which is the basis of all Nature. The law of polarity is that law according to which everything attains completion by manifesting itself in the opposite direction to that from which it started. It is the simple law by which there can be no inside without an outside, nor one end of a stick without an opposite end.

———————————~————————

Our subconscious assumptions continually externalize themselves that others may consciously see us as we subconsciously see ourselves, and tell us by their actions what we have subconsciously assumed of ourselves to be. Therefore let us assume the feeling "I AM Christ," until our conscious claim becomes our subconscious assumption that "We all with open face beholding as in a glass the glory of the Lord are changed into the same image from glory to glory." Let God Awake and his enemies be destroyed. There is no greater prayer for man.

If I strive to be master, I shall never attain; if I aim to be, I shall never arrive; if I look up and away to a power outside and beyond Myself, I shall never find. Only when I know as I AM known shall I find that I, Self, the Jesus Christ character, am Master. I, the one Life, the one Intelligence, am Spirit, Truth. I, the one and the all, the unborn and the undying, AM the Power and the Glory, the living Reality.

──────────── ∼ ────────────

Our behavior is influenced by our subconscious assumption respecting our own social and intellectual rank and that of the one we are addressing. Let us seek for and evoke the greatest rank, and the noblest of all is that which disrobes man of his morality and clothes him with uncurbed immortal glory. Let us assume the feeling "I AM Christ," and our whole behavior will subtly and unconsciously change in accordance with the assumption.

God is I AM That I AM, and you are I AM, and you make your destiny and your own fate by the things which you attach to that I AM, for that is what you really believe about yourself. If you give credence to fear by saying, "I AM afraid," then you are destroying yourself. Every time you entertain a pang of fear, or jealousy, or a thought of criticism, every time you speak an unkind word to anyone, and much more so if you say it about them when they are not present, you are definitely shortening and destroying your life. You are definitely breaking down your cells. You are making your body more sensitive to pain. Nor do we lose a grain of good. Nobody can keep it away from you. Every time you say, "I AM one with God," you are improving your life. Every time you refuse to be bullied by fear, every time you follow the highest you know, and put your trust in God, you are lengthening your life, improving your health, and making it more difficult for disease to attack you.

The Power of "I AM"

Man has made no more important discovery than this law. It opens an era in human progress that presages the realization of that New Civilization which prophets have foreseen and sages foretold. This Law is the one Principle, present in every New Thought movement. The Law is stated thus, I AM THAT WHICH I THINK I AM. Every person is controlled by his thoughts. The mental attitude determines conditions of body and environment.

———————————

Begin to affirm, "I AM strong. I AM radiant. I AM happy. I AM inspired. I AM illumined. I AM loving. I AM kind. I AM harmonious." Feel these states of mind; affirm them, and believe them; then you will begin to truly live in the Garden of God.

Creation is finished. You call your creation into being by feeling the reality of the state you would call. A mood attracts its affinities but it does not create what it attracts. As sleep is called by feeling "I AM sleepy," so, too, is Jesus Christ called by the feeling, "I AM Jesus Christ." Man sees only himself. Nothing befalls man that is not the nature of himself. People emerge out of the mass betraying their close affinity to your moods as they are engendered. You meet them seemingly by accident but find they are intimates of your moods. Because your moods continually externalize themselves you could prophesy from your moods, that you, without search, would soon meet certain characters and encounter certain conditions. Therefore call the perfect one into being by living in the feeling, "I AM Christ," for Christ is the one concept of self through which can be seen the unveiled realities of eternity.

The Power of "I AM"

The Universe is One. This Universe is divided, by my Consciousness, into myself and that which is not myself. This division is purely a mental one; I make it when I say, "I AM"; this means there is a manifestation of the Universe which I AM not. That which I AM not is named variously: God, Energy, Force, Nature, etc. Names cannot change IT. They are names, and names are symbols only for that which is. I AM in the Universe, not a portion of it, but I AM a manifestation of IT. Thus my recognition of Self divides the Universe, to my consciousness, into what I call "I," which is the Within, and what I call "Not I," which is the Without. This is the simplest of all philosophy. It is as simple as Cause and Effect.

Subjectively, as a manifestation of Unity, man is potential power in every direction. In the objective life he is unfolding that which he is in the subjective. Being all potential power, why should he not affirm that power? Why limit the manifestation of the subjective "I AM" to the little power he has heretofore manifested? There is no reason, except habit Let him say henceforth: "I possess, and, since, by thinking I have power to direct the manifestations of the subjective life I AM, I affirm that I AM power to do that which I desire to do!" He who will so affirm, will do. If I AM one with the highest, I AM the highest, for God and man cannot be separated. The kingdom is within.

———————⌇———————

It does not matter what the appearances round about you are like. All things make way for the coming of the Lord. I AM the Lord coming in the appearance of that which I AM conscious of being. All the inhabitants of the earth cannot stay my coming or question my authority to be that which I AM conscious that I AM.

The Power of "I AM"

Your I AMness, your Consciousness, is the way in which you change your world. Whatever you attach to I AM you become. As you affirm with feeling, I AM illumined, inspired, loving, harmonious, peaceful, happy and strong, you will resurrect these qualities that lie dormant within you, and wonders will happen in your life. When men and women help you in the realization of your dreams, they are playing their part and are messengers testifying to your beliefs and convictions. You wrote the play, and other men and women execute the parts conforming to your concept of yourself.

―――――――――∼――――――――

The Top Secret

When you say "I AM," you are announcing the Presence of God within you, as explained in the third chapter of Exodus. "I AM" means Pure Being, Life, Awareness, Self Originating Spirit, Unconditioned Consciousness. In other words, it is a secret to millions of people, because they don't know that when they say "I AM," they are proclaiming the Presence of God within them. It is called "Om" in India, and many chant the word "Om" as a mantra. It is important that you know the meaning of the word "Om" before using it. In Sanskrit, mantra means an instrument of thought.

Woman is a continuing symbol throughout the Bible for this reason: Woman stands for the human soul. From a metaphysical point of view the Woman is not just Eve, or Mary, or Jezebel, or any particular person. Woman signifies the human soul your soul . . or as psychology expresses it, the psyche or mind. That is represented by Woman, and the history of Woman in the Bible is the history of your soul, and one of the keys to your destiny.

The soul is not the divine part of you. This divine part is the "I AM," "Pneuma," which we will consider later. Your soul expresses itself as your personality, and that includes everything in the conscious and subconscious mind. So it is the changing personality, the psyche, which is represented by Woman in the Bible.

The whole of history is really the story of the human soul, always changing, either getting better or getting worse. It is a receptive thing . . this constant change in your thought . . as you either allow the spiritual power, the "I AM," to govern, or you let the lower self have sway. So, WOMAN IS THE SOUL.

The Power of "I AM"

It is not, I will be master, but it is, I AM master. It is not, I will succeed, but it is, I AM success. It is not, I will have health, but it is, I AM health, wholeness, perfection. I AM all life, all intelligence, all good, all glory, for the only "I" there is, is "I AM That I AM." God, Father, Son, Christ, Jesus, Life, I, Intelligence, Soul, Spirit, Love, Being, One, Totality, are synonymous terms, all meaning ,the one God, the one I AM, for besides this, there is none else.

———————————~———————————

So when you say, "I AM poor, sick or weak; I AM not one with the Creative Mind," you are using that creative power to keep yourself away from the Infinite; and just as soon as you declare that you are one with God, there is a rushing out to meet you, as the Father rushed out to meet the prodigal son. "The Spirit seeketh," but as long as your mind thinks in the terms of conditions you cannot overcome. The difficulty comes from our inability to see our own Divine nature, and its relation to the Universe. Until we awake to the fact that we are one in nature with God, we will not find the way of life; until we realize that our own word has the power of life we will not see the way of life; and this brings us to the consideration of the use of the Word in our lives.

The Power of "I AM"

There is something within us that is greater than things, and it is our privilege to claim the power of that something now. "I have overcome the world now, and every soul may live in Me now." That means emancipation now for all who will receive it. Freedom is not for some other world, but for the life we are living today. We are not required to live in tribulation at any time during present existence; the way to complete emancipation is before us at all times. I AM the way. Whoever will transcend personal consciousness and enter into the consciousness of "I AM" will enter that life that is not of this world, and he will gain that power that can overcome anything that may exist in this world.

———————————～———————————

Think of the bigness of things in the universe, think of the number of grains of sand, the profusion of all life, and never again limit anything. All is yours to use. Jesus would never have become the Christ unless he had had the courage to say, "Behold, I AM He." You will never attain until in some degree you are able to say the same thing of yourself.

The Power of "I AM"

This Power that now moves through us in its Ninth Dimension of Divine Universal Brotherhood is invisible, dynamic and dramatic in its ability to create from the invisible Source held within its own heart. It is self sustaining, self renewing, and nothing is impossible to it. It contains the invisible Substance to mold into all outer creations, just as the atom holds invisible Power within itself. Nothing on earth can withstand the irresistible movement of this mighty Power or its ability to change every cell, every condition, every thought and action into itself. It is already perfect, and it can and does absorb all imperfections into itself as it moves, forth, undiluted by man's ignorance and unhindered by man's interference. This is the Mind of God in action as man. It is a miracle. Our thinking, our desires and our plans must change the instant we move up to where it is found. We contact this Power when we move into our own Garden of Eden, the "I AM" center of consciousness, where this Almighty Power of God embraces and enfolds us.

If you contemplate Me, the I AM, as the God within, then you will know that the limitations of the human personality are broken. Be still. Let me reveal myself to you . . in a way which will cause you to know the Allness of the Kingdom here and now.

33

Jesus established the identity of the Father as man's awareness of being. "I and My Father are one, but My Father is greater than I". I AM one with all that I AM conscious of being. I AM greater than that which I AM aware of being. The creator is ever greater than his creation.

——————————~——————————

So long as the Word exists the thing will exist, for since the Word is All Power there is nothing beside It. "I AM That I AM, and beside me there is none other." This "I AM" is Spirit, God, All. There is no physical explanation for anything in the universe; all causation is Spirit and all effect spiritual. We are not living in a physical world but in a spiritual world peopled with spiritual ideas. We are now living in Spirit.

The Power of "I AM"

No matter how kind and useful I make my conduct toward an individual, if in my secret heart I AM criticizing him severely and condemning him, I must expect criticism and condemnation from others as my portion.

———————— ～✓ ————————

My superconscious mind is the essence and form of the Infinite in me. It is that part of me which is pure Divinity. In this Superconscious Self the perfect pattern of my life is wrought. All my efforts in living a good life help to bring this divine pattern into expression through the subconscious, out into conscious expression. That is the purpose of my life, to bring this slumbering divinity deep within the soul of me into expression in all my ways. This is the purpose of all life. Affirmations and efforts to do good give this divinity, this I AM of me, a chance to express over all the negative conditions of the subconscious and conscious parts of me.

Each person is a movement of Infinity on the screen of space. You gravitate to your parents according to the tone or mood of parents at the moment of conception. In other words, you are the Infinite Spirit appearing as a child in the home of your parents. Quimby said it correctly when he said, "You are a Spirit now. You were always a Spirit. When will you cease to be a Spirit?" You are conditioned as John Jones to believe yourself to be a man of age, carpenter, American, etc. Actually, you are I AM (God) appearing in the form of man of a certain age, race and profession. It is the One Being appearing as many. Mozart's father didn't have to know music. The I AM within you produces anything and everything.

Commands, to be effective, must be to oneself. "I AM That I AM" is the only effective command. "I AM the Lord and beside Me there is none else". You cannot command that which is not. As there is no other, you must command yourself to be that which you would have appear.

The Power of "I AM"

"I of myself can do nothing," . . the mind, the body, the form, the character in the dream, the picture on the screen can do nothing. But I AM, which is All-in-all, which is without beginning and end, . . this "I" is Truth and can do all because it is all.

———————————～———————————

I AM the way, and you are that I AM; you must be or you could not be one with the Father. If you are not that I AM you would be separated from God, and no soul can be separate from God and live. Claim your divine sonship; claim your divine inheritance; claim that supreme power that overcomes the world; it belongs to you; it is you; know this truth and this truth shall make you free.

Eliminate all negative thoughts that come into your mind. Yet do not spend all your time in denials but give much of it to the clear realization of the everywhere present and waiting substance and life. Some of us have in a measure inherited "hard times" by entertaining the race thought so prevalent around us. Do not allow yourself to do this. Remember your identity, that you are a son of God and that your inheritance is from Him. You are the heir to all that the Father has. Let the I AM save you from every negative thought. The arrows that fly by day and the pestilence that threatens are these negative race thoughts in the mental atmosphere. The I AM consciousness, your Savior, will lead you out of the desert of negation and into the Promised Land of plenty that flows with milk and honey.

The Power of "I AM"

The One and Only Power

The Bible calls this Power, I AM, which means Being, life,
awareness, unconditioned consciousness, Self Originating
Spirit. All things are made by the self contemplation of Spirit,
or God. It creates by Itself, becoming the thing It creates.
"Before Abraham, was I AM". This means before any
objectification or manifestation of ideals or desires takes
place, the unconditioned or formless awareness . . I AM . .
conditions Itself into the image and likeness of your concept
or ideal.

You think you lack love, money, home, etc., but what you really lack is the consciousness of God . . I AM. If He were dwelling in your thoughts continually these things would be added. Jesus did not worry about hotel accommodations when he went from place to place, he simply knew that "the upper chamber" was always ready for him. All things are mental before they are expressed in the material. Then speak the word out: "My word shall not return unto me void, but shall accomplish whereunto it is sent."

———————— ~~~ ————————

The I AM can never be coerced or robbed of its perfect freedom, and all attempts in that line will meet with final disaster. When we have once decided to return to the Father's house, to regain this lost estate within, it is an easy road. It may seem hard at the start, because we have to throw away so much baggage, but it grows easier as we get closer and closer to the great heart of the loving Father. A Helper has been provided, the "Spirit of truth . . shall guide you into all the truth"; all we have to do is to seek honestly and sincerely to enter in. "Seek, and ye shall find; knock, and it shall be opened unto you." This promise is to everyone.

The works are finished. All that is required of you to let these qualities into expression is the claim . . I AM That. Claim yourself to be that which you desire to be and that you shall be. Expressions follow the impressions, they do not precede them. Proof that you are will follow the claim that you are, it will not precede it.

The "I AM" within you, which means Being, Life, Awareness, Self Originating Spirit, etc. is God, or the Life Principle. "I AM" is the true Christmas tree, and all gifts are on the Christmas tree, for God is both the giver and the gift. If you work for someone and he pays you, he is liquidating an obligation; but "I AM" is a gift to you. No work or sacrifice is needed.

But it is wonderfully simple when you understand it. You are demonstrating the so-called fall of man every time you lose yourself in the whirl of sense pleasure. The mission of the I AM is happiness. It seeks joy and bliss; they are set before it in unstinted measure, and it revels in their intoxicating draughts, but the mastery of the higher mind should ever be maintained.

———————————~——————

The symbol of the ring is to emphasize the importance of changing the focus of man's belief from matter and external conditions to Spirit, the Cause of all. Isaiah stresses the great truth that there is only One Power of creation, and it is I AM, or consciousness, awareness, mind or imagery. There is no other creative power. Your mind must reach an absolute conviction regarding the One Power, which is beyond all argument, disputation and comparison; then you reach a point of real faith and confidence, which is your rest in God

The Power of "I AM"

The I AM has its being in heaven; its home is in the realm of perfect ideals, the Christ within, but it has its freedom. It loves to be. To be is to enjoy. To enjoy is for the time to be that which we enjoy. When you are absorbed in the recital of an interesting story, you are lost to all else. The I AM is for the moment identified with that which it enjoys. Here is the solution of a great mystery . . how the I AM ever came to separate itself from its sphere of wisdom.

———————~——

What is the lost word, the secret Name of God in you? I AM. This is the great secret of the so called lost word. This is the philosopher's stone of the alchemists, and it is really the secret lying behind all religious and all philosophies.

Chapter 8 of the Book of John . . and John reports the highest teaching of Jesus . . gives a good deal of insight concerning the cosmic nature of the I AM. Jesus was teaching in the temple, in the part called the treasury, and he began to speak to the crowd, saying, "I AM the light of the world. He that followeth me [my teaching] shall not walk in darkness, but shall have the light of life." The Pharisees immediately took exception, claiming he was bearing false testimony of himself. Jesus patiently explained that he was not speaking of his own mind but as he was inspired by the Father. But they would have none of it. As Jesus himself said, there are none so blind as those who will not see.

I AM is expressed through I will; it is the business of I AM to know when the I will activities are ideally true. In its right relation in Being, I AM never possesses or owns anything. All things in the universe are its to use, but it must not claim them as personal property.

The Power of "I AM"

Do you go out to see a man with a reputation, or run after a book that is said to contain the key? When you realize that the I AM within you is the KEY to every person, place, and thing, you will begin to unlock the treasures of your own kingdom. You will then be able to release the hidden springs of inspiration in a book or within your soul, and see the new life fill everything.

———————～————

If you have been accustomed to feeling prejudices and dislikes easily, you will not all at once find it easy to illustrate your assertion, "I AM love." If you have indulged yourself in thoughts of disease, the old aches and pains will intrude even while you say "I AM health!"

I, as a spiritual being, AM a temple of the living Creator. There are three courts to my temple: the outer court, which is my conscious mind, the middle court, which is the subconscious, and the inner court, the superconscious, the holy of holies. When I affirm, I AM love for all humanity;

or:

I consecrate my life to the healing of humanity, or any other statement of truth , I AM endeavoring to bring the potentiality of my superconscious mind out into expression in my conscious life. By the constant repetition of affirmations of goodwill, and the persistent practice of unselfish living, I AM gradually unfolding the beauty that is hidden within, and making it an actuality in this world.

The Power of "I AM"

Spiritual man is I AM; manifest man is I Will. I AM is the Lord God of Scripture; and I Will the Adam. It is the I AM man that forms and breathes into the I Will man the "breath of life." When we are in the realm of the ideal we are I AM; when we are expressing those ideals in thought and act we are I Will. When the I Will gets so absorbed in its realm of expression that it loses sight of the ideal, and centers all its attention upon the manifest, it is Adam listening to the serpent, and hiding from the Lord God. This breaks the connection between Spirit and manifestation, and man loses that consciousness of harmony which is his under Divine Law. Then to keep up manifestation, there is a drawing upon the reserve forces of the organism, or tree of life; and the real source of supply being cut off, man is figuratively described as driven out of the Garden of Eden, or Paradise of Being.

The Power of "I AM"

By the constant repetition of affirmations of goodwill, and the persistent practice of unselfish living, I AM gradually unfolding the beauty that is hidden within, and making it an actuality in this world.

I AM superior to all negative thoughts and influences. As I AM joyous and radiant with creative thoughts, I attract the radiant life.

You will become aware that there is something greater and nobler and more enduring in you than in all this splendid display of creative activity spread before your eyes. You will feel it true that the intelligence in you which can say I AM and I WILL is like that Great I AM, that Omnipotent Will, which governs the universe. Henceforth life will have a new meaning to you. You will begin to grow in the power of individuality. The Great I AM is the unceasing affirmation and expression of Infinite Love, Wisdom and Power.

The Power of "I AM"

The will plays the leading part in all systems of thought concentration. The simple statement, I will to be well, gathers the forces of mind and body about the central idea of wholeness, and the will holds the center just so long as the I AM continues its affirmation. No one ever died until he let go his will to live, and thousands live on and on through the force of a determined will.

———————————～～————————————

"I AM the Lord; that is My name; and My glory will I not give to another". "I AM the Lord, the God of all Flesh". This I AM within you, the reader, this awareness, this consciousness of being, is the Lord, the God of all Flesh. I AM is He that should come; stop looking for another. As long as you believe in a God apart from yourself, you will continue to transfer the power of your expression to your conceptions, forgetting that you arc thc conceiver. The power conceiving and the thing conceived are one but the power to conceive is greater than the conception.

"Whom do you say that I AM?". This is not a question asked two thousand years ago. It is the eternal question addressed to the manifestation by the conceiver. It is your true self, your awareness of being, asking you, its present conception of itself, "Who do you believe your awareness to be?" This answer can be defined only within yourself, regardless of the influence of another. I AM (your true self) is not interested in man's opinion. All its interest lies in your conviction of yourself. What do you say of the I AM within you? Can you answer and say, "I AM Christ"? Your answer or degree of understanding will determine the place you will occupy in life. Do you say or believe yourself to be a man of a certain family race, nation etc.? Do you honestly believe this of yourself? Then life, your true self will cause these conceptions to appear in your world and you will live with them as though they are real.

The Power of "I AM"

The problem of self control is never settled until all that man is comes into touch with the divine will and understanding. You must understand all your forces before you can establish them in harmony. This overcoming is easy if you go about it in the right way. But if you try to take dominion through will, force, and suppression, you will find it hard and will never accomplish any permanent results. Get your I AM centered in God, and from that place of Truth speak true words. In this way you will gain real spiritual mastery and raise your will consciousness from the human to the divine.

———————⌒〜——————

You are God. You are the "I AM That I AM". You are consciousness. You are the creator. This is the mystery, this is the great secret known by the seers, prophets, and mystics throughout the ages.

The Power of "I AM"

Never say, "I don't know," "I don't understand." Claim your Christ understanding at all times, and declare: I AM not under any spell of human ignorance. I AM one with infinite understanding. The accumulation of ignorance gathered through association with ignorant minds can be dissolved by using the word. You may know by simply holding the thought that you know. This is not egotism, but spiritual knowing. When you declare divine understanding, you sometimes meet your old line of thought and are disappointed. Right then continue to hold to your declaration for knowing. Judge not by appearances. Do not act until you get the assurance; if you keep close to Spirit by affirmation, the assurance will come. Will it come by voice? No! You will know through the faculty of intuition. Divine knowing is direct fusion of mind of God with mind of man. Sometimes we are taught by symbols, visions, and the like, but this is only one of the ways that Divine Mind has of expressing itself. When the mind deals with God ideals it asks for no symbols, visible or invisible, but rests on pure knowing. It was in this consciousness that Jesus said: "Father, I thank thee that thou heardest me. And I knew that thou hearest me always."

The Power of "I AM"

Make your daily assertions, "I AM love, health, wisdom, cheerfulness, power for good, prosperity, success, usefulness, opulence." Never fail to assert these things at least twice a day; twenty times is better. But if you do not attain to all immediately, if your life does not at once exemplify your words, let it not discourage you. The saying of the words is the watering of the seeds. After a time they will begin to sprout, after a longer time to cover the barren earth with grain, after a still longer time to yield a harvest.

———————— ～～ ————————

Your I AM is a center of radiance in the source of supply. You are a magnet! You are an image of the Great Magnet, the omnipotent Will that holds the universe in form! You can attract from the soul and nature of the universe all that you need for the growth of your own I AM. There is no limit to the supply. It is equal to your demand. It will manifest for your use as you learn how to express and exercise the magnetic powers of your mind. Your affirmations enable you to call forth from your soul and to individualize the qualities and powers of this Great Magnet.

Creative thought uses the will to build up individual consciousness. The Lord God, or Jehovah, of Genesis, is the original "I WILL BE THAT I WILL BE." In mind, both Jehovah and Jesus mean I AM. I AM is man's self identity. I AM is the center around which man's system revolves. When the I AM is established in a certain understanding of its Principle, it is divinely guided in its acts, and they are in harmony with divine law.

If man's concept of himself were different, everything in his world would be different. His concept of himself being what it is, everything in his world must be as it is. Thus it is abundantly clear that there is only one I AM and you are that I AM. And while I AM is infinite, you, by your concept of yourself, are displaying only a limited aspect of the infinite I AM.

The Power of "I AM"

"Prove me and see if I will not open the windows in heaven and pour out a blessing you will not be able to receive." Where is heaven? It is a state of consciousness. What is the ME? It is the I AM within you, and hence the windows that are to be opened are in your own consciousness, and the blessings that are to be poured out are the ideas which will pour out through your own mind into the manifest world of expression. It is wonderful. Millions and millions of blessings are yours. Do You hear, Son of God?

———————⌇~⌇/———————

Man should constantly affirm: I AM, and I will manifest, the perfection of the Mind within me. The first part of the statement is abstract Truth; the second part is concrete identification of man with this Truth. We must learn the law of expression from the abstract to the concrete . . from the formless to the formed. Every idea makes a structure after its own image and likeness, and all such ideas and structures are grouped and associated according to their offices.

55

Finally, to press home the point that he was not referring to Jesus the man but to the cosmic Christ, he said to them, "If ye believe not that I AM He, ye shall die in your sins." Here we have one of those words in the Bible which are printed in italics. This occurs whenever a word was missing in the original manuscript, and the translators put it in italics to show that the word was supplied by them. However, in this case the word "he" was not in the original. The translators erroneously inserted it, thinking it was necessary grammatically to complete the sentence. But Jesus is not speaking about himself. He is saying that unless a person believes in the I AM, the Indwelling Christ in every man, he has misunderstood his relationship to God, and he will die without knowledge of the Word of Power. Jesus continues this thought by saying, "When ye have lifted up the Son of man, then shall ye know that I AM He, and I do nothing of myself; but as my Father hath taught me [inspired me], I speak these things." Again the italicized word was erroneously inserted. The meaning here is that when we come to a true understanding of man's relationship to God, then we shall know that I AM is the presence of God in each one, and that that presence gives dominion.

The Power of "I AM"

I AM That I AM. I AM the formless awareness of being conceiving myself to be man. By my everlasting law of being I AM compelled to be and to express all that I believe myself to be.

———————— ⌇ ————————

I AM the eternal Nothingness containing within my formless self the capacity to be all things. I AM That in which all my conceptions of myself live and move and have their being, and apart from which they are not. I dwell within every conception of myself; from this withinness, I ever seek to transcend all conceptions of myself. By the very law of my being, I transcend my conceptions of myself, only as I believe myself to be that which does transcend. I AM the law of being and beside ME there is no law. I AM That I AM.

I AM; man's unconditioned awareness of being is revealed as Lord and Creator of every conditioned state of being. If man would give up his belief in a God apart from himself, recognize his awareness of being to be God (this awareness fashions itself in the likeness and image of its conception of itself), he would transform his world from a barren waste to a fertile field of his own liking. The day man does this he will know that he and his Father are one, but his Father is greater than he. He will know that his consciousness of being is one with that which he is conscious of being, but that his unconditioned consciousness of being is greater than his conditioned state or his conception of himself.

***

"Be still and know that I AM God".

Yes, this very I AM, your awareness of being, is God, the only God. I AM is the Lord . . the God of all Flesh . . all manifestation.

The Power of "I AM"

Your world is your consciousness objectified. Waste no time trying to change the outside; change the within or the impression; and the without or expression will take care of itself. When the truth of this statement dawns upon you, you will know that you have found the lost word or the key to every door. I AM (your consciousness) is the magical lost word which was made flesh in the likeness of that which you are conscious of being.

———————————⟋⌒⟍⟋———————————

God and the world both give to us just what we demand of them, just what we claim with unwavering faith as rightfully ours. When we seek first the kingdom of God and its right-living; when the "I AM" is in the seat of dominion, and draws all things to Itself by the power of love and the law of attraction, then all good is ours, and ours Now. An unselfish service thinks not of reward; the love which prompts it is its own reward. There must be no belief in lack along any line; we must not think or talk about lack, but affirm abundant supply. This will bring to the one who faithfully follows the practice, the fullness of all he needs.

The Power of "I AM"

"Whatsoever ye shall ask in My name, that will I do". This certainly does not mean to ask in words, pronouncing with the lips the sounds, God or Christ Jesus, for millions have asked in this manner without results. To feel yourself to be a thing is to have asked for that thing in His name. I AM is the nameless presence. To feel yourself to be rich is to ask for wealth in His name. I AM is unconditioned. It is neither rich nor poor, strong nor weak. In other words, in HIM there is neither Greek nor Jew, bond nor free, male nor female. These are all conceptions or limitations of the limitless, and therefore names of the nameless. To feel yourself to be anything is to ask the nameless, I AM, to express that name or nature".

I dwell within every conception of myself; from this withinness, I ever seek to transcend all conceptions of myself. By the very law of my being, I transcend my conceptions of myself, only as I believe myself to be that which does transcend. I AM the law of being and beside ME there is no law.

The Power of "I AM"

Your unconditioned awareness or I AM is the Virgin Mary who knew not a man and yet, unaided by man, conceived and bore a son. Mary, the unconditioned consciousness, desired and then became conscious of being the conditioned state which she desired to express, and in a way unknown to others, became it. Go and do likewise; assume the consciousness of that which you desire to be and you, too, will give birth to your savior. When the annunciation is made, when the urge or desire is upon you, believe it to be God's spoken word seeking embodiment through you. Go, tell no man of this holy thing that you have conceived. Lock your secret within you and magnify the Lord, magnify or believe your desire to be your savior coming to be with you.

———————————～——————

The study of spiritual science will connect you consciously with the constructive, healing power of the Creator and in that process the All Person will become much more to you than an abstract Principle of Power. You will come to know the I AM as an actual, real, creative Intelligence in every cell of your nature, in every thought of your mind, in every emotion of your feelings and in every motion of your will.

On rising in the morning be as particular in plunging into your bath of joy as you are in taking your usual bath in water. Say over to yourself, "I AM filled with joy; I AM in an atmosphere of joy." Make your atmosphere so joyous that all who come near you will feel its buoyancy.

I raise my mind from all appearances of limitation to the consciousness of the one Omnipotent Power and affirm that I AM the recipient of all its goodness and love.

If you find it difficult to declare that you are well when you are feeling sick, then just assume that you are a perfect being in a perfect world, enjoying a perfect experience. Act as though I were and ye shall know I AM. The miracle working radiance will take hold of you, will transform you, . . and you will behold that which ought to be is! You, yourself are the fulfillment of all that you wish, all that you desire. You cannot possibly conceive of any joy or any experience which it would be impossible for you to fulfill.

———————————————

The good news is that there is a direct relationship between the amount of responsibility you accept and the amount of control you feel. The more you say, "I AM responsible!" the more of an internal locus of control you develop within yourself, and the more powerful and confident you feel.

The Power of "I AM"

Said Jesus, "Your father Abraham rejoiced to see my day: and he saw it, and was glad. Then said the Jews unto him, thou art not yet fifty years old, and hast thou seen Abraham?" Jesus ended his dissertation, saying, "Verily, verily, I say unto you, Before Abraham, was I AM." Jesus was giving emphasis to the mystical nature of the I AM. It is the Cosmic Christ which has always existed but which came to its fullest expression in the person of Jesus. I AM is the eternal self which was never born and will never die.

———————◇———————

The mentality is not God, is not divine Mind, is not cause. It makes neither good nor evil. Yet, mind would like to announce to the world: "I AM a seat of importance. I can kill with wrong thoughts, and I can heal with right thoughts. Man is according to the way I AM thinking. If I AM thinking evil, then man is evil; if I AM thinking good, then man is good. I make the man, for it has been repeatedly uttered that man is the way I, mind, am thinking, that my thinking makes the man what he is. I put the man up or I pull the man down. Some men are afraid of me while others worship me; some call me error and evil and devil, while others having respect for me, call me power and intelligence, yes, and even call me God."

The Power of "I AM"

"Be Still, and Know That I AM God." Suddenly, for the first time I began to see or hear what BE STILL meant. It is a letting go of every desire . . every wish or idea . . a blankness. When this is established, the Power of God has the unobstructed way of expression and comes through into manifestation. Manifestation is the last stage. It is action in non-action . . when there is no "think" action in this inactivity of the personal, the Divine comes into manifestation. Not to fulfill the wishes and desires and ideas I had treasured for a lifetime, but to bring out the things that "eye hath not seen." It is a discovery that reality, which has been trying to come through for so long, is about to express itself with ease and naturalness.

"I AM the light of the world", crystallizing into the form of my conception of myself. Consciousness is the eternal light, which crystallizes only through the medium of your conception of yourself. Change your conception of yourself and you will automatically change the world in which you live. Do not try to change people; they are only messengers telling you who you are. Revalue yourself and they will confirm the change.

Just imagine! You can free yourself from negative emotions and begin taking control of your life by simply saying, "I AM Responsible!" whenever you start to feel angry or upset for any reason.

You must recognize, "I AM He that should come," and know that once and for always you are not looking for another, and, strange as it may be, the moment you find this within your own consciousness you find it everywhere and in everybody, and in everything and place, yet confined to none . . yet containing them all. This is Oneness, Wholeness, and God.

The Power of "I AM"

The best spiritual medicine today is to get acquainted with the Spirit within you and then claim peace, harmony, and Divine law and order in your life. Reflect and dwell upon the Divine Law, which is: "I AM That which I contemplate." Contemplate whatsoever things are true, lovely, noble and Godlike and let wonders happen in your life.

———————— ∾ ————————

The best and quickest way to bring about reform in our thinking is by the use of a strong affirmation, to be repeated in the Silence and any time the need arises. The following: "I AM healthy, strong, young, powerful, loving, harmonious, successful, and happy"

All things are made by God (consciousness) and without him there is nothing made that is made. Creation is judged good and very good because it is the perfect likeness of that consciousness which produced it. To be conscious of being one thing and then see yourself expressing something other than that which you are conscious of being is a violation of the law of being; therefore, it would not be good. The law of being is never broken; man ever sees himself expressing that which he is conscious of being. Be it good, bad or indifferent, it is nevertheless a perfect likeness of his conception of himself; it is good and very good. Not only are all things made by God, all things are made of God. All are the offspring of God. God is one. Things or divisions are the projections of the one. God being one, He must command Himself to be the seeming other for there is no other. The absolute cannot contain something within itself that is not itself. If it did, then it would not be absolute, the only one. Commands, to be effective, must be to oneself. "I AM That I AM" is the only effective command.

The Power of "I AM"

A few months ago, I said in one of my Sunday morning lectures at the Saddleback Theatre in El Toro that whatever a person added to "I AM" with feeling and understanding would come to pass. One man said to himself, "I AM going to try it."

Accordingly, many times a day he would affirm, out loud when possible, "I AM prosperous. I AM healthy. I AM happy. I feel wonderful!" Driving along the road his silent speech was the same. He made a habit of it and found it to be a valid law of life. His business, his health and his relationship with his family have undergone a marked transformation. He discovered that his changed attitude changed everything in his life.

If God's name forever and forever is I AM, how can you look outside of self? You cannot point to another and say: "I AM." You can observe this or do that, but you cannot point to another when you say: "I AM."

Keep in mind that when you pray about any specific thing, it is necessary to qualify your mind with the consciousness or feeling of having or being that thing. You mentally reject completely the arguments in your mind against it; that is prayer. Qualify your consciousness with the thing you are praying for by thinking about it with interest Do this quietly and regularly until a conviction is reached in your consciousness. As you do this, the problem will no longer annoy you. You will maintain your mental poise, plus the feeling of: "I now feel that I AM what I long to be," and as you continue to feel it, you will become it.

Your whole world may be likened to solidified space mirroring the beliefs and acceptances as projected by a formless, faceless presence, namely, I AM. Reduce the whole to its primordial substance and nothing would remain but you, a dimensionless presence, the conceiver.

The Power of "I AM"

You have entered the spiritual world, and I AM the door to that world; you have risen to that supreme state of being where you can say, in the spirit of eternal truth, I AM, and through the power of that truth you have overcome the world.

———————⌒—————

Here is the law: "I AM That which I feel myself to be." Practice changing the feeling of "I" every day by affirming: "I AM Spirit; I think, see, feel, and live as Spirit, the Presence of God. (The other self in you thinks, feels, and acts as the race mind does.) As you continue to do this, you will begin to feel you are one with God. As the sun in the heavens redeems the earth from darkness and gloom, so will the realization of the Presence of God in you reveal the man you always wished to be . . the joyous, radiant, peaceful, prosperous, and successful man whose intellect is illumined by the Light from above.

The Power of "I AM"

To develop individuality, the first essential is to give the "I AM" its true and lofty position in your mind. The "I AM" is the very center of individuality, and the more fully conscious you become of the "I AM" the more of the power that is in the "I AM" you arouse, and it is the arousing of this power that makes individuality positive and strong. Another essential is to practice the idea of feeling or conceiving yourself as occupying the masterful attitude. Whenever you think of yourself, think of yourself as being and living and acting in the masterful attitude. Then in addition, make every desire positive, make every feeling positive, make every thought positive, and make every action of mind positive. To make your wants distinct and positive, that is, to actually and fully know what you want and then proceed to want what you want with all the power that is in you, will also tend to give strength and positiveness to your individuality; and the reason is that such actions of mind will tend to place in positive, constructive action every force that is in your system.

The Power of "I AM"

Perhaps it may sound a little strange to you at first to say that you are Tom Brown or Mary Jones, the Christ; but then, every new thing seems strange at first. Later you will say to yourself, Why did I not recognize that long ago? When there is a problem that seems difficult to solve, think to yourself, "I AM so and so, the Christ." Then think what that means. Can the Christ be sick? Can the Christ be in lack? Can the Christ be stymied by any problem? Of course, if you are going to refer to yourself as Tom Brown or Mary Jones, the Christ, it will be necessary for you to give more than lip service. Your actions must also be in accord with that high ideal. There is power in your true name when you know how to use it. I AM That I AM is the Great Name, and I AM is the greatest name short of that.

The Power of "I AM"

When man develops the "I AM" consciousness, he will attain the realization of what he is now; he will discern that his present nature is limitless in possibility, and that the conscious possession of more and more of the richness of his nature will come, not from more and more years of development, but from more and more present realization.

———————————$\sim$———————————

We frequently hear the expression, "I can never do anything right," and it is quite simple to understand that such a mode of thought would train the mind to act below its true ability and capacity. If you are fully convinced that you can never do anything right, it will become practically impossible for you to do anything right at any time, but on the other hand, if you continue to think, "I AM going to do everything better and better," it is quite natural that your entire mental system should be inspired and trained to do things better and better.

The Power of "I AM"

Who Are You?

Look at your spiritual heritage. We are all children of the I AM, as Moses says. Within you is the real nature or the real name, because you are pronouncing it all day long. I AM. It is called Om in India. The Bible says, I AM That I AM. Moses said, I AM hath sent me unto you.

———————⌇———————

"But," one protests, **"how can I believe I AM perfect** when I AM so lame that I cannot take a step; when I AM full of pain; when I have such evil thoughts; when I AM afraid?" Let one say, "I AM perfect; there is no sick man in heaven. There is no evil in heaven." Let him say it over and over, and something will begin to burn in him; something will begin to believe that it is true; and softly, like the breath of the morning breeze, something will whisper to him, "Yea, Yea, it is so!" Then with the warmth and the fire that is burning and blazing, his belief will burst into the love of clear understanding; and he will come into intelligent discernment of God and man.

There is only one power and this power is God (consciousness). It kills; it makes alive; it wounds; it heals; it does all things, good, bad or indifferent. Man moves in a world that is nothing more or less than his consciousness objectified. Not knowing this, he wars against his reflections while he keeps alive the light and the images which project the reflections. "I AM the light of the world". I AM (consciousness) is the light. That which I AM conscious of being (my conception of myself) . . such as "I AM rich", "I AM healthy", "I AM free" . . are the images. The world is the mirror magnifying all that I AM conscious of being.

The Power of "I AM"

In a preceding chapter, it was stated that the "I AM" is the ruling principle in man, and from that statement the conclusion may be drawn that the "I AM" is the ruling power as well, but this is not strictly correct. There is a difference between principle and power, though for practical purposes it is not necessary to consider the abstract phase of this difference. All that is necessary is to realize that the "I AM" directs the mind, and that the power of the mind directs and controls everything else in the human system. It is the mind that occupies the throne but the "I AM" is the power behind the throne. This being true, it becomes highly important to understand how the power of the mind should be used, but before we can understand the use of this power, we must learn what this power actually is.

The Power of "I AM"

We are all children of the I AM (God). Whatever you attach to I AM, you become. If you say, "I AM no good, I'm a flop, I'm a failure, I'm going deaf, I'm going blind, I'm nobody," then you become what you affirm. Therefore, reverse it and say, "I AM happy, joyous and free. I AM illumined; I AM inspired. I AM strong; I AM powerful. `Let the weak say, I AM strong.' `Let the widow say, it is well.' I AM a son or daughter of the Living God. I AM heir to all of God's riches. I AM born to win and to succeed, for the Infinite cannot fail. I AM a tremendous success. I AM absolutely outstanding. I AM unique, and there is no one in all the world like me."

Why don't you claim the above and write these truths in your heart and inscribe them in your inward parts? He that hath an ear, let him hear what the Spirit saith unto the churches. . . To him that overcometh will I give to eat of the hidden manna, and will give him a white stone, and in the stone a new name written, which no man knoweth saving he that receiveth it.

The Power of "I AM"

ALL DAY LONG and every day, the God in You keeps repeating . . "I AM." But He lets YOU end the sentence. You can add "poor" or "rich", "sad" or "happy", "sick" or "well," as YOU choose. God can do for you only what you ALLOW Him to do THROUGH you. You praise and bless Him, only when you see the good and true and beautiful. You dishonor Him when you call yourself weak or sick or poor.

———————————— ~~~ ————————————

I AM a revelator of the Living Word . . I AM the revelator of the Living Word . . and I AM, therefore, not surprised that the thing decreed shall come to pass. A stone thrown into the air will certainly come down without any aid from the one who threw it; so the word of the revelator will certainly return to him freighted with results, and he will not have to care about its return . . that will automatically take place. "My own shall come unto me" . . by a sure and certain way. Why worry, then?

The Power of "I AM"

Dare you to say . . "Every day In every way I AM getting richer and richer"? If you dare . . and will follow up the word with the mental image of yourself HAVING all the riches you desire . . Spirit substance will make your word manifest and show you the way to riches.

———————⌒——————

When illumination lights your consciousness, it breaks forth like a burning flame into all your affairs. We have been taught to say, "My business is a success. My business succeeds and prospers," but with insight, we no longer work for a successful business after this fashion, for this would be casting down our vision, it would be looking at the image and attempting to control it by certain means of the mind. With insight, we announce, "I AM success," for it is Self that is the success and not the business. Is this clear to you? When you know who you are and why you are, then you know yourself as you are known, and you understand intelligently that because of your being, you are inherently a success, and it is said of you, "All that thou doest shall prosper."

The Power of "I AM"

The trouble with many people is this: When they pray, they are tense, anxious, and impatient. They say, "I wonder when it will come?" Others say, "Why has it not happened yet? If I say, "Why?" it means I AM anxious and lack faith. If I know a thing is true, I do not question my prayer. Let us remember, therefore, anytime we ask, "Why?" to ourself or another, it means we have not reached a conviction within ourselves. When we possess something in consciousness, we do not seek it; we have it! Another point I want to stress here is: When the student questions, "How will it come?" he shows lack of faith and conviction. By illustration, I AM now in Los Angeles, I do not ask, "How will I get there?" I AM there. Similarly when our ideal is fixed in consciousness, we do not wonder, "How will I get there?" I AM there already. Where your consciousness is, you are. "Where I AM there you will be also."

───────── ∿ ─────────

Any expression that is not felt is unnatural. Before anything appears, God, I AM, feels itself to be the thing desired; and then the thing felt appears. It is resurrected; lifted out of the nothingness. I AM wealthy, poor, healthy, sick, free [or] confined were first of all impressions or conditions felt before they became visible expressions.

I AM He. Right now, I AM overshadowing you, the reader, my living temple, with my presence, urging upon you a new expression. Your desires are my spoken words. My words are spirit and they are true and they shall not return unto me void but shall accomplish where unto they are sent ["So shall my word be that goeth forth out of my mouth: it shall not return unto me void, but it shall accomplish that which I please, and it shall prosper in the thing whereto I sent it". They are not something to be worked out. They are garments that I, your faceless, formless self, wear. Behold! I, clothed in your desire, stand at the door (your consciousness) and knock. If you hear my voice and open unto me (recognize me as your savior), I will come in unto you and sup with you and you with me ["Behold, I stand at the door, and knock: if any man hear my voice, and open the door, I will come in to him, and will sup with him, and he with me". Just how my words, your desires, will be fulfilled, is not your concern. My words have a way ye know not of. Their ways are past finding out.

The Power of "I AM"

We can so fill ourselves with the drawing power of attraction that it will become irresistible. Nothing can hinder things from coming to the man who knows that he is dealing with the same power that creates all from itself, moves all within itself, and yet holds all things in their places. I AM one with the Infinite Mind. Let this ring through you many times each day until you rise to that height that, looking, sees.

———————～———————

When we accept an idea from another mind, or from our own study simply because it seems plausible, we will permit that idea to impress itself upon the subconscious, provided it is deeply felt. Later on that same idea will come back from the subconscious as a strong conviction; and we shall not only be forced to accept it as true, but in addition it will color all our thinking; in fact, it may become so strong that we do not care to be free from its absolute control. There are many illustrations of this very thing, as there are quite a number of people who are in such complete bondage to the mental control of the beliefs they cherish that they actually take pride in being under such absolute control; in brief, they frequently declare, "I AM completely in the hands of this system of thought and I AM glad of it."

The Power of "I AM"

By example if you want to be a singer on the radio, imagine you are before a microphone; the microphone is now in front of you, and you see the imaginary audience; you are the actor. ("Act as though I AM, and I will be.") You feel yourself into the situation; you are singing now (in your imagination); enter into the joy of it; feel the thrill of accomplishment! Continue to do this in your imagination until it begins to feel natural for you; then go off to sleep. If you have succeeded in planting your desire in your subconscious mind, you will feel a great sense of peace and satisfaction when you awaken. An interesting thing will have happened: You will have no further desire to pray about it, because it is fixed in consciousness. The reason for this is that the creative act has been finished, and you are at rest.

———————⁓———————

"I AM alpha and omega, the beginning and the end, saith the Lord." Our ideal murmuring in our hearts is the alpha; in order that it become the omega, we must enter into the feeling that it is ours now, and walk the earth knowing that it is so.

Listen carefully to the promise, "Ye shall not need to fight in this battle: Set yourself, stand still, and see the salvation of the Lord with you". With you! That particular consciousness with which you are identified is the Lord of the agreement. He will without assistance establish the thing agreed upon on earth. Can you, in the face of the army of reasons why a thing cannot be done, quietly enter into an agreement with the Lord that it is done? Can you, now that you have found the Lord to be your awareness of being, become aware that the battle is won? Can you, no matter how near and threatening the enemy seems to be, continue in your confidence, standing still, knowing that the victory is yours? If you can, you will see the salvation of the Lord. Remember, the reward is to the one who endures. Stand still. Standing still is the deep conviction that all is well; it is done.

No matter what is heard or seen, you remain unmoved, conscious of being victorious in the end. All things are made by such agreements, and without such an agreement, there is not anything made that is made. "I AM That I AM".

Truth does no work. Truth knows. One must at such times merely let his light shine. That which is true does not change from better to worse or from worse to better, and one is to know changeless being. Instead of going to the mind for instruction as a student might approach his teacher for knowledge, you are the instructor yourself, and you are to speak to your mind living words, teaching the mind I AM the power of the Truth. Always know that you are the teacher of your mind, that your mind comes to you for orders, that your mind must be obedient to fort and that you are not at the mercy of your mind.

———————～————————

You must have no master or lord but . . I AM . . God . . The One Power. We must categorically and emphatically mentally reject all other powers but the One Primal Cause, the Spirit within. If we have a master, we are slaves. This is why He says, "Call no man master." Man is not a serf. He has been given dominion. When we are convinced beyond a shadow of a doubt that our own I AMness is our Lord and Master, we know no other and we are free.

The Power of "I AM"

"Be still and know that I AM God," takes on a new meaning: Be still and assume the glories of this new estate. Assume them in the secret place . . easily, naturally; assume them and rest them in the silence. "Be wise as serpents . . harmless as doves." Know nothing, see nothing, hear nothing, then you will know all, see all, and hear all.

It is impossible to serve two masters at the same time. The master man serves is that which he is conscious of being. I AM Lord and Master of that which I AM conscious of being. It is no effort for me to conjure poverty if I AM conscious of being poor. My servant (poverty) is compelled to follow me (conscious of poverty) as long as I AM (the Lord) conscious of being poor. Instead of fighting against the evidence of the senses, you claim yourself to be that which you desire to be. As your attention is placed on this claim, the doors of the senses automatically close against your former master (that which you were conscious of being). As you become lost in the feeling of being (that which you are now claiming to be true of yourself), the doors of the senses once more open, revealing your world to be the perfect expression of that which you are conscious of being.

The Power of "I AM"

Life is strong, and you are strong with the strength of the Infinite; forget all else as you revel in this strength. You are strong and can say I AM. You have been laboring under an illusion; now you are disillusioned. Now you know, and knowing is using the law in a constructive way. "I and my Father are One;" this is strength for the weak, and life for all who believe.

***

Another important essential is to affirm silently in your own mind that you are the "I AM," and as you affirm this statement or as you simply declare positively, "I AM" think of the "I AM" as being the ruling principle in your whole world, as being distinct and above and superior to all else in your being, and as being you, yourself, in the highest, largest, and most comprehensive sense. You thus lift yourself up, so to speak, to the mountain top of masterful individuality; you enthrone yourself; you become true to yourself; you place yourself where you belong. Through this practice you not only discover yourself to be the master of your whole life, but you elevate all your conscious actions to that lofty state in your consciousness that we may describe as the throne of your being, or as that center of action within which the ruling "I AM" lives and moves and has its being.

The Power of "I AM"

If you merely think of yourself as Tom Brown or Mary
Jones with your aches and pains and bills to pay, you are
not thinking with power. But if you say, "I AM Tom Brown,
the Christ," or "I AM Mary Jones, the Christ," then you are
identifying yourself with the Eternal and the good. Now,
make no mistake, you are not saying you are Jesus, the
Christ. You are simply voicing your true identity as a child of
God, Tom Brown or Mary Jones, the Christ. This is your new
name which only you can use. It is fulfilling the prophecy
which Jesus made, "The works that I do shall ye also do. . .
Is it not written in your law, I said, Ye are gods?" Thus Jesus
becomes the great diagram for living, and I AM is the Way by
which we can follow", him in a personal demonstration of the
Christ.

———————~~——————

Have we spoken "I AM" upward, toward the good, or
downward toward the not good? That which we have been
receiving will tell the story. Jesus said that if they asked
rightly in His name, their "joy would be made full." Is your
joy full? If not, then give heed to your asking.

The Bible compares the opinionated man to the camel who could not go through the needle's eye. The needle's eye referred to was a small gate in the walls of Jerusalem, which was so narrow that a camel could not go through it until relieved of its pack. The rich man, that is the one burdened with false human concepts, cannot enter the Kingdom of Heaven until relieved of his burden any more than could the camel go through this small gate. Man feels so secure in his manmade laws, opinions and beliefs that he invests them with an authority they do not possess. Satisfied that his knowledge is all, he remains unaware that all outward appearances are but states of mind externalized. When he realizes that the consciousness of a quality externalizes that quality without the aid of any other or many values and establishes the one true value, his own consciousness. "The Lord is in His holy temple". Consciousness dwells within that which it is conscious of being. I AM is the Lord and man, his temple. Knowing that consciousness objectifies itself, man must forgive all men for being that which they are. He must realize that all are expressing . .without the aid of another . . that which they are conscious of being.

The Power of "I AM"

God is Pure Spirit, Infinite Mind, and Infinite Intelligence. The Bible calls the Name of God, "I AM," meaning Pure, Unconditioned Being. No one can, of course, define God, for God is Infinite, but there are certain Truths which the illumined of all ages have perceived as true of God, and that is why the Bible says, "I AM That I AM." What is "I AM?" It is your True Being . . your Real Self; nobody can say, "I AM," for you. That is the Presence of God in you, and your Real Identity. Whatever you affix to "I AM," and believe, you become. Always claim, "I AM strong, powerful, radiant, happy, joyous, illumined, and inspired"; then you are truly practicing the Presence, for all these qualities are true of God.

————————～⁓————————

Jesus also said, "If ye shall ask anything of the Father, he will give it you in my name" . . that is, in the name I AM. Whenever you desire . . not supplicate, but desire, speaking the "I AM" upward . . He will give what you ask. Every time you say, "I AM happy," you ask in His name for happiness. Every time you say, "I AM unhappy," you ask in His name for unhappiness.

If you wish to control and direct the forces you possess, you must act from the throne of your being, so to speak or in other words, from that conscious point in your mental world wherein all power of control, direction and initiative proceeds; and this point of action is the center of the "I AM." You must act, not as a body, not as a personality, not as a, mind, but as the "I AM," and the more fully you recognize the lofty position of the "I AM," the greater becomes your power to control and direct all other things that you may possess. In brief, whenever you think or act, you should feel that you stand with the "I AM," at the apex of mentality on the very heights of your existence, and you should at the same time, realize that this "I AM" is you . . the supreme you. The more you practice these methods, the more you lift yourself up above the limitations of mind and body, into the realization of your own true position as a masterful individuality; in fact, you place yourself where you belong, over and above everything in your organized existence.

The Power of "I AM"

On another occasion, when Jesus came into Caesarea Philippi, he questioned his disciples, "Whom do men say that I the Son of man am?" In other words, "Who do the people think I AM?" And his disciples replied, "Some say that thou art John the Baptist; some, Elias; and others, Jeremias, or one of the prophets." In passing, it should be noted that the people of that day had a strong belief in reincarnation, for they were in fact saying that Jesus was a reincarnation of one of the prophets. And then Jesus turned the question to the disciples themselves. "But whom say ye that I AM?" And Simon Peter answered and said, "Thou art the Christ, the Son of the living God." And Jesus answered, "Blessed art thou, Simon Barjona: for flesh and blood hath not revealed it unto thee, but my Father which is in heaven." Jesus could say, and did, "I AM the Christ," and so can you. Each one has a secret name known to God, and when you get your inspiration, your illumination, you will receive a new name. In Revelation we read, "To him that overcometh will I give . . . a white stone, and in the stone a new name written, which no man knoweth saving he that receiveth it."

"Come up higher" . . you come up higher by being still and knowing that I AM (in midst of you) is God . . by recognizing your own divinity . . the Father within as a point where God can and does flow through into manifestation easily, naturally, unemotionally . . automatically. It cannot be otherwise.

———————~——————

By reason of the precious revelation of Jesus Christ . . "I AM the Truth, etc." do you see that all the impersonal qualities of God can be embodied and become personal? Hence instead of using Love you are LOVE . . "I AM That I AM" what I AM? . . I AM Love . . Truth . . Light, . . and with each acceptance it comes into manifestation automatically in accordance with the degree of your recognition.

The Power of "I AM"

Timothy, said: "Let everyone that nameth the name of the Lord depart from unrighteousness." Let everyone who speaks the "I AM" keep it separated from iniquity, or from false speaking. Let it be spoken always upward, never downward.

———————～——————

The day man feels "I AM free", "I AM wealthy", "I AM strong", God . . I AM . . is touched or crucified by these qualities or virtues. The results of such touching or crucifying will be seen in the birth or resurrection of the qualities felt, for man must have visible confirmation of all that he is conscious of being. Now you will know why man or manifestation is always made in the image of God. Your awareness imag[in]es and out pictures all that you are aware of being. "I AM the Lord and besides me there is no God". "I AM the Resurrection and the Life".

Just as the law of gravity existed long before Newton became aware of it, so the Power of the Christ existed before Jesus, and "Before Abraham was . . I AM." It is wonderful when you begin to perceive life and to know that is not something that was invented within the last hundred years, trademarked, copyrighted, and earmarked by a thousand personalities, all claiming the right to be the discoverer of God. In the realm of Spirit there is no "personal" brand on God. You may write your initials in fire on the side of a steer and show your possession, but trying to make a personal possession of God shows a feeble understanding of the Infinite. If God is all, what then is the protection thrown up about the discoveries of Him?

The "I AM" is fundamentally conscious: that is, the "I AM" knows what exists in the human field or in the human sphere and what is taking place in the human sphere; and that constitutes consciousness. In brief, you are conscious when you know that you exist and have some definite idea as to what is taking place in your sphere of existence.

The Power of "I AM"

At the spoken word of Jesus the invisible became visible . . the unseen, unsuspected substance, which like the wind "listeth where it bloweth," condensed into visible manifestation. The WORD is the condenser . . when this word is Spoken from the consciousness that "I AM That I AM" . . that particular I AM or Temple . . or Manifestation, should come into this particular situation and disintegrate the congested human thought which has made all sorts of evil pictures. It is not precipitation which is often referred to as a "top flight" indication of Secret Power. It is a natural releasing into a plane of physical sight and hearing, that which has always been.

———————～———————

We are ever that which is defined by our awareness. Never claim, "I shall be that". Let all claims from now on be, "I AM That I AM". Before we ask, we are answered. The solution of any problem associated with desire is obvious. Every problem automatically produces the desire of solution.

Though I heal ten thousand cases of diseases and cause them to disappear from the body, and though countless times, I change the mind from one idea to another, if I AM unaware that I have thereby accomplished nothing I know not Truth. Though I transform thoughts into things and things into thoughts ten thousand times and know not that in doing this nothing has taken place in reality, I know not Truth. When my mind is placid like a crystal lake, my mind fulfills itself, reflects like a mirror the Intelligence which I AM.

———————⁓———————

The I AM in you is the Presence of God, Awareness, Pure Being, The Living Spirit, the Creator of all things visible and invisible. This is why every man is his own savior. Truth is saying to you to break away from all beliefs that instill fear into your mind

The Power of "I AM"

Man is schooled in the belief that his desires are things against which he must struggle. In his ignorance, he denies his savior who is constantly knocking at the door of consciousness to be let in (I AM the door). Would not your desire, if realized, save you from your problem? To let your savior in is the easiest thing in the world. Things must be, to be let in. You are conscious of a desire; the desire is something you are aware of now. Your desire, though invisible, must be affirmed by you to be something that is real. "God calleth those things which be not (are not seen) as though they were". Claiming I AM the thing desired, I let the savior in.

———————～———————

Before Abraham or the world was . . I AM. When all of time shall cease to be . . I AM. I AM the formless awareness of being conceiving myself to be man. By my everlasting law of being I AM compelled to be and to express all that I believe myself to be.

I AM a spiritual and mental magnet attracting to myself all things, which bless and prosper me.

———————~⁄———————

Your consciousness or your I AM is the unlimited potential upon which impressions are made. I'm-pressions are defined states pressed upon your I AM. Your consciousness or your I AM can be likened to a sensitive film. In the virgin state, it is potentially unlimited. You can impress or record a message of love or a hymn of hate, a wonderful symphony or discordant jazz. It does not matter what the nature of the impression might be; your I AM will, without a murmur, willingly receive and sustain all impressions.

The Power of "I AM"

Suffering from maladjustments and internal bodily trouble, the path of freedom lies within the recognition of this automatic, involuntary Power already there. The dropping of everything from thought and the entering into this recognition, will right the condition with the speed commensurate to your recognition . . and rising from a sick bed you will be able to say with authority "I AM Well" . . and mean it.

———————～〜———————

To enter the supreme life of the Christ is to gain the supreme power of the Christ; and to steadily grow in the consciousness of that life and power is to rise out of every tribulation until complete emancipation has been gained. That supreme life is in store for us; it already exists in the supreme "I AM" of our own being; this "I AM" is the Son of God, the only begotten of God, the Christ in us; and the Christ that is in each one of us is one with each one of us. That is how "I AM in the Father, and ye in me."

But everyone can develop this state of conscious possession of his whole self by remaining firm in the conviction that "All that I AM is mine." When you begin to feel that you possess yourself you actually have something in consciousness, and according to the laws of gain and possessions you will gain more and more without end. You are in the same consciousness with those who have, and to you will be given. You have established the inner cause of possession through the conscious possession of your entire inner life, and the effect of this cause, that is, the perpetual increase of external possession, must invariably follow. In brief, you have applied the great law "To Him That Hath Himself All Other Things Shall Be Given".

I AM an open door for all that I AM to enter.

My awareness of being magnifies all that I AM aware of being, so there is ever an abundance of that which I AM conscious of being. It makes no difference what it is that man is conscious of being, he will find it eternally springing in his world. The Lord's measure (man's conception of himself) is always pressed down, shaken together and running over. There is no need to fight for that which I AM conscious of being, for all that I AM conscious of being shall be led to me as effortlessly as a shepherd leads his flock to the still waters of a quiet spring.

The Power of "I AM"

The laws which now hold you in bondage to material things will perish (have no power over you) when you have come to an understanding of Spirit. "Ye shall know the truth, and the truth shall make you free," said Jesus. As in the case of stomach trouble so in every case of inharmony whatsoever, you must work to overcome fear; "I will fear no evil; fevers, colds, contagion, heredity, signs, superstitions, have no power to harm me." If you would be free, declare your freedom positively, with understanding. By mastering the principle of being, you will be enabled to apply the principle, thus freeing yourself. The "I AM" is the true self, the God within. As long as you say "I AM discouraged," and name over different kinds of diseases that affect your body in different parts, you are making laws against yourself; "Out of the heart of man proceed evil thoughts;" and by affirming on the negative side you put off the day of your freedom. Your word goes out and returns to you in the form you gave it. You sent out the words, "I AM sick," and your word vibrates through your system, carrying your decree to every atom of your being.

The Power of "I AM"

Now that my memory is restored . . so that I know I AM the Lord and beside me there is no God . . my kingdom is restored. My kingdom . . which became dismembered in the day that I believed in powers apart from myself . . is now fully restored. Now that I know my awareness of being is God, I shall make the right use of this knowledge by becoming aware of being that which I desire to be.

What we speak of as form, is everything in the organized personality that has shape and that serves in any manner to give expression to the forces within us. In the exercise of consciousness, we find that the "I AM" employs three fundamental actions. When the "I AM" looks out upon life we have simple consciousness. When the "I AM" looks upon its own position in life we have self consciousness, and when the "I AM" looks up into the vastness of real life we have cosmic consciousness.

Henceforth, stop using the "Truth" . . exchanging this old worn out profitless habit for the Wisdom . . "I AM the Truth" . . From that elevation of consciousness everything you say or do is automatically blessed . . so it is also with the LIGHT . . I do not use it . . I AM the LIGHT" . . there is a vast difference in the results that will follow. And of course "I AM The WAY" I do not demonstrate it any more. If you contemplate the difference in "knowing the Truth" and "being the Truth" you will see the distinct advantage of this.

———————⌇———————

Every feeling makes a subconscious impression and, unless it is counteracted by a more powerful feeling of an opposite nature, must be expressed. The dominant of two feelings is the one expressed. I AM healthy is a stronger feeling than I will be healthy. To feel I will be is to confess I AM not; I AM is stronger than I AM not. What you feel you are always dominates what you feel you would like to be; therefore, to be realized, the wish must be felt as a state that is rather than a state that is not.

The Power of "I AM"

I AM the vine, ye are the branches. Whatever you attach to I AM, you magnify. I AM magnifies every state of mind. For example, if you say, "I AM poor, I AM lonesome, I AM miserable," you magnify those mental conditions.

───────── ～～ ─────────

The First Commandment, "Thou shalt have no other gods before me," is an admonition to look to one source for our good and it indicates that Me or I AM is that source. To this law all must render obedience. I AM the one who must obey it. If I lived in the constant awareness of my true identity, it would be impossible for anyone to interfere with my demonstration of harmonious, fruitful and eternal life, and if men always heeded the First Commandment, the journey into the Kingdom of God would be a quick one.

"I AM the good shepherd and know My sheep and am known of Mine. My sheep hear My voice and I know them and they will follow Me". Awareness is the good shepherd. What I AM aware of being is the 'sheep' that follow me. So good a 'shepherd' is your awareness that it has never lost one of the 'sheep' that you are aware of being.

———————～———————

I AM nameless, but will take upon Myself every name (nature) that you call Me. Remember, it is you, yourself, that I speak of as 'me'. So every conception that you have of yourself . . that is every deep conviction you have of yourself . . is that which you shall appear as being; for I AM [is] not fooled; God is not mocked.

The Power of "I AM"

The I AM within you, which means Being, Life, Awareness, Self Originating Spirit, etc.. is God, or the Life Principle. I AM is the true Christmas tree, and all gifts are on the Christmas tree, for God is both the giver and the gift. If you work for someone and he pays you, he is liquidating an obligation; but I AM is a gift to you. No work or sacrifice is needed.

Peace is now. The God of peace is within you and you can claim it. Love is now. Open your mind and heart to the influx of Divine love now, for God is the Eternal Now! Power is now, poise is now and joy is now. The Healing Presence is within you, and you can claim that the Infinite Healing Presence is flowing through you now, this very minute. The answer to your problem, whatever it is, is within you now, for Infinite Intelligence knows all things.

. . Before they call, I will answer. God is timeless, spaceless and ageless. Take your good now. You might as well claim all your good now as to do so a hundred years from now. Why wait?

"Since the beginning man cried aloud, 'Who am I?' "And My Voice forever answers, Thou Are I. I, the Universal One, am thou whom thou art creating in My image. "I AM I. I AM I whom I AM creating. I AM the universal I.

———————⌇———————

It is said, "You believe in God. Believe also in Me, for I AM He". Have the faith of God. "He made Himself one with God and found it not robbery to do the works of God". Go you and do likewise. Yes, begin to believe your awareness, your consciousness of being to be God. Claim for yourself all the attributes that you have heretofore given an external God and you will begin to express these claims. "For I AM not a God afar off". I AM nearer than your hands and feet . . nearer than your very breathing. I AM your awareness of being. I AM That in which all that I shall ever be aware of being shall begin and end. "For before the world was, I AM; and when the world shall cease to be, I AM"; "before Abraham, was I AM". This I AM is your awareness.

The Power of "I AM"

"God is in his heaven . . all is well with the world." "The Kingdom of Heaven is at hand" "The Kingdom of Heaven is within you." Only believe, and all things are yours. "Now is the accepted time" . . right now, while you are reading this. Right now while I AM writing "is the accepted time" to bring about realization, to live it, to sing it, to go about our Father's business, using his inexhaustible supply. Absence of God in our thoughts is the only thing that can keep away demonstration. Where God is, there is an abundance of all things he feeds us on his ideas.

Reject the evidence of your senses which mock your assumption, and you take the father and mother of the child into your mind, which means your I AMness. This is the Father and Mother of all creation, your Awareness, or Consciousness. As you claim and feel you now are what you long to be, the condition which you desired and assumed to be true becomes objectified in your world and bears witness to your inner conviction.

'

But knowing this law by which a man transforms himself,
I assume that I AM what I want to be and walk in the assumption that it is done. In becoming it, the old man dies and all that was related to that former concept of self dies with it. You cannot take any part of the old man into the new man. You cannot put new wine in old bottles or new patches on old garments. You must be a new being completely. As you assume that you are what you want to be, you do not need the assistance of another to make it so. Neither do you need the assistance of anyone to bury the old man for you. Let the dead bury the dead. Do not even look back, for no man having put his hand to the plow and then looking back is fit for the kingdom of heaven. Do not ask yourself how this thing is going to be. It does not matter if your reason denies it. It does not matter if all the world round about you denies it. You do not have to bury the old. "Let the dead bury the dead." You will so bury the past by remaining faithful to your new concept of Self that you will defy the whole vast future to find where you buried it. To this day no man in all of Israel has discovered the sepulchre of Moses.

The Power of "I AM"

If one says to himself, "I AM filled with life, health, strength and vigor," and then goes down the street saying, "I see a poor blind beggar, a criminal and a sick person," he is still treating himself just as much as when he affirmed that he was perfect. We are only as perfect as we perceive others to be. This does not mean that we shut our eyes to those who are in trouble; for we may have sympathy with the one having trouble without having sympathy with his trouble.

———————～⁓/———————

Under my direction, he reversed this image and practiced the mirror treatment every morning for about five or ten minutes. He looked in the mirror and affirmed out loud: "I AM all health. God is my health." Gradually, the idea of wholeness entered into his subconscious mind, and he is now free from a false belief. He practiced the technique I gave him diligently and faithfully until it manifested in his life.

"I AM the Lord, and there is no God beside Me" declares
my consciousness to be the one and only Lord and beside my
consciousness there is no God. When we learn that "I AM the
door," and seek this door in the spiritual life within us, we
shall find it; and as we pass through this door we enter the
other side of life, the divine side, the eternal side. There we
find the kingdom of God that is within us, and beyond is the
shining shore. But we are not required to leave the personal
form and the physical life in order to live on the other side of
life. True being is to live on the spiritual side of life and to
manifest the perfection of spiritual being in the personal side
of life. Thus the Word becomes flesh and the glory of God is
made visible in man.

Man's thoughts constitute a veritable universe. A man
and a woman in love with each other will grow into a single
harmony; . . if we love God by tuning in and claiming his
attributes, we will grow into His likeness and then will not
feel it robbery to do the works of God. Man is God walking
the earth, but man has forgotten it. We really tune in with
our Higher Self when we tune in with God. The man who
sings the Song of the Lamb (I AM Christ) is the man of
tomorrow.

The Power of "I AM"

My savior is my desire.

As I want something I AM looking into the eyes of my savior. But if I continue wanting it, I deny my Jesus, my savior, for as I want I confess I AM not and "except ye believe that I AM He ye die in your sins." I cannot have and still continue to desire what I have. I may enjoy it, but I cannot continue wanting it.

There is but the one I AM That I AM. There is not one big "I" and millions of smaller "I's." One Life is all there is, even as one air is all the air there is. This one I AM That I AM includes granite heights, crystals, trees, flowers, birds, animals, man, and all created things. Surrender, therefore, the ifs, buts, whys and wherefores for this absolute state of yourself . . your radiant I AM, ever the Self revealing Light.

The I AM does not concern itself with your sins or limitations, with your past or future. Does not concern itself with your body or affairs; with your father or mother, your husband or wife; with your station in life, your color, age nor education. The I AM concerns itself only with you. Ever it declares, There is no cause or effect besides Me; I see no ignorance or darkness, no evil, anywhere, for to Me there is nothing but Myself. I AM the All in all.

115

The Power of "I AM"

I AM found when all else fails; when all other means are of no avail; and when no thinking can find the way out. Lo, your extremity is my opportunity to prove to you Myself to be your All-in-all. I AM present always, the never failing, Self existent One. If you make your bed in hell, lo, I AM there. If you take the wings of the morning and dwell in the uttermost parts of the sea, ever there I AM, for I AM with you wherever you are. I AM your Self.

I AM the Self which, apparently, you have wandered away from . . but only as in a dream which you can readily see, if you will, has no substance at all. No dream can ever separate us, for I AM with you wherever you are. I AM with you in your sorrow, in your failure, in your defeat. I AM with you in your joy, in your pleasure, in your success. What is darkness to you shineth as the light to me.

I AM the Self to whom you now lovingly turn. None of your delusions affect Me. Ever I AM at your side waiting only your awareness of Me, your recognition and realization of Me as your All-in-all, to set you free from any false belief in separation. When you leave all for Me, then shall you find Me. When you cry out yearningly from your heart to Me, then shall you hear My voice answering you. I AM your hope of Glory. I AM your bright and morning Star. I AM the Lord, your God. I AM YOU, your Self.

"Make straight the way of the Lord" simply means the state that is to come in desire. We clear the way for it by removing all obstacles such as doubt, fear and idle thoughts. "I baptize with water." Water will assume the shape of any vessel into which it is poured. Water, therefore, means unconditioned consciousness which is all things to all men. When we use the I AM, we condition consciousness by believing. Think emotionalized thoughts "I AM sick, I AM old, I AM tired," and these emotionalized ideas become fixed states, i. e. are poured into a vessel and assume its shape. Water is a cleansing agent; we cleanse or purge consciousness from sin, from a mistake or limitation by assuming a new mood or cultivating a new idea in our mind, and thrilling to it, it finally becomes a conviction within us.

------------∽------------

As I stand here, having discovered that my consciousness is God, and that I can by simply feeling that I AM what I want to be transform myself into the likeness of that which I AM assuming I AM; I know now that I AM all that it takes to scale this mountain.

The Power of "I AM"

And I have declared unto them thy name, and will declare it: that the love wherewith thou hast loved me may be in them, and I in them. This means that all through the ages teachers have declared the Truth: I AM the Lord, I AM the door, and I AM is the only law of consciousness. Millions of years from now this Truth will still be declared, until mankind becomes aware of the being he really is. As this love of Truth is made known to the individual, he loves this Eternal Principle and enjoys sharing this Divine secret with his brother man. Sooner than we think will the Fatherhood of God and the brotherhood of man be made manifest in this entire earth conscious planet.

"I AM hath sent me" reveals my consciousness to be the Lord which sends me into the world in the image and likeness of that which I AM conscious of being to live in a world composed of all that I AM conscious of. "I AM the Light of the world" . . that is all you need to recognize in order to clear any darkened veil of human belief from your eyes. It is wonderful to contemplate the Power of the Presence and the Word in the midst of you.

The "I AM" does not depend upon thought or feelings, times or places, conditions called sin and goodness, life and death, for its existence: the I AM That I AM says, I AM all power, I AM all perfection. Do not confine Me to this or that idea or thought, word or saying. Do not limit Me to churches or ministers, to man or woman, to books or sentences. I AM That I AM, the Unconditioned, the Eternal One.

———————— ~~~ ————————

The conceiver and the conception are one. If your conception of yourself is less than that which you claim as true of God, you have robbed God, the Father, because you (the Son or conception) bear witness of the Father or conceiver. Do not take the magical Name of God, I AM, in vain for you will not be held guiltless; you must express all that you claim yourself to be. Name God by consciously defining yourself as your highest ideal.

The Power of "I AM"

The name Jehovah was given to the people thousands of years ago and later written down in the Bible, in order that people might know they are one with God, to know that God is the ever-present help waiting to redeem and save. It is the knowledge that the love of God shines through and says, "I AM your God and you are my people. I AM That I AM but you are I AM, my beloved son in whom I AM well pleased." Jesus knew the Power of the I AM and he used it in many constructive ways. "I AM the good shepherd . . I AM the door ... I AM the bread of life. I AM the way, the truth, and the life." These expressions were commonplace in his everyday teaching. But there were occasions when he gave special significance to the I AM, emphasizing its mystical quality.

———————⁓———————

The question "Whom do you say that I AM?" is not addressed to a man called "Peter" by one called "Jesus". This is the eternal question addressed to one's self by one's true being. In other words, "Whom do you say that you are?". For your conviction of yourself . . your opinion of yourself . . will determine your expression in life. He states, "You believe in God . . believe also in Me". In other words, it is the Me within you that is this God.

The Power of "I AM"

This is Jesus' simple message to man: Men are but garments that the impersonal being, I AM, the presence that men call God . . dwells in. Each garment has certain limitations. In order to transcend these limitations and give expression to that which, as man . . John Smith . . you find yourself incapable of doing, you take your attention away from your present limitations, or John Smith conception of yourself, and merge yourself in the feeling of being that which you desire. Just how this desire or newly attained consciousness will embody itself, no man knows. For I, or the newly attained consciousness, has ways that ye know not of "I have meat to eat that ye know not of", its ways are past finding out. Do not speculate as to the HOW of this consciousness embodying itself, for no man is wise enough to know the how. Speculation is proof that you have not attained to the naturalness of being the thing desired and so are filled with doubts.

The great truth is that our own I AMness (consciousness) can resurrect and make visible that which we accept and feel as true within. Your own consciousness has the power to resurrect you from any state of limitation.

Does the Christ Self exist because of what you, personally, think or feel? Does the Real man, or man in his Real state know about Spirit and flesh, good and bad, or about time and place, sin, sickness and death? What is it that the I AM knows? It knows I AM, and besides Me there is none else! It knows, "I AM in the Father, and the Father in Me." Thus I AM ever one with the I AM That I AM. Say it over and over, sing it softly to yourself . . I AM That I AM. Lovingly, earnestly, expectantly. Do not attempt to define what it means, nor analyze your feeling, but just say it, and it will begin to reveal itself to you, for the I AM That I AM reveals Itself to me, to you, to all who say, I will arise and go unto my Self in my true state of being . . where nothing can oppose me . . nothing!

The Power of "I AM"

Your answer to, "Whom do you say that I AM"? ever determines your expression. As long as you are conscious of being imprisoned or diseased or poor, so long will you continue to out picture or express these conditions. When man realized that he is now that which he is seeking and begins to claim that he is, he will have the proof of his claim. This cue is given you in words, "Whom seek ye?". And they answered, "Jesus". And the voice said, "I AM He". 'Jesus' here means salvation or savior. You are seeking to be salvaged from that which is not your problem. "I AM" is He that will save you. If you are hungry, your savior is food. If you are poor, your savior is riches. If you are imprisoned, your savior is freedom. If you are diseased, it will not be a man called Jesus who will save you, but health will become your savior. Therefore, claim "I AM He", in other words, claim yourself to be the thing desired. Claim it in consciousness . . not in words . . and consciousness will reward you with your claim. You are told, "You shall find Me when you FEEL after Me" . . "And ye shall seek Me, and find Me, when ye shall search for Me with all your heart". . . Well, FEEL after that quality in consciousness until you FEEL yourself to be it. When you lose yourself in the feeling of being it, the quality will embody itself in your world.

The Great "I AM." . . Revealed to Moses as the One and Only Real Mind or Power in the Universe. That beside Which there is no other. I AM is another way of saying God. The "I AM" in man is the Life of man; without this "I AM," man could not be.

The I AM That I AM is the infinite Power House wherein the ever existent good is generated and maintained. According to Genesis, God declared: "Let the earth bring forth grass . . Let the waters bring forth the moving creatures . . Let the earth bring forth the living creatures. And it was so." The command, you see, was definitely stated for the desired thing. Let there be this particular thing! "And it was so."

The Power of "I AM"

When you make a declaration, affirmation or statement of what you wish to do, or what you desire to bring to pass, remember this paramount fact: spiritual things must be spiritually conceived and brought forth. Therefore, when you think, do not feel that it is a human mind you are using with which to bring about some special good, but as the man of God, the I AM Self, know that you are thinking with the Christ Mind and you will inevitably bring forth what is rightfully yours. Then your Word, spoken as by the divine Mind, is your authority that it shall not return to you void, but shall go forth and multiply your good. This was Jesus' authority, and likewise may be yours.

The soul, or the "I AM," already has within itself everything that is good, and if you would have all of these good things from within express themselves in your personality, you must think and live right. You must think the truth and think it constantly. Before there can be action in the without there must be thought in the within, and as is the thought within so will be the action without.

Then Jesus said, "Ye shall know the truth, and the truth shall make you free." This statement covers many facets of man's life, but in this context it has a special meaning. The Bible says that there were those in the crowd who answered, "We be Abraham's seed, and were never in bondage to any man: how sayest thou, Ye shall be made free?" Jesus told them they were judging after the flesh but if they would change their minds and understand that the Son . . the I AM . . has all power, then they would be free indeed and no longer have to rely upon intermediaries, or upon some supposed good that came out of the past.

The Power of "I AM"

Because I AM (your consciousness) is the resurrection and the life, you must attach this resurrecting power that you are to the thing desired if you would make it appear and live in your world. Now you begin to assume the nature of the thing desired by feeling, "I AM wealthy"; "I AM free"; "I AM strong". When these 'FEELS' are fixed within yourself, your formless being will take upon itself the forms of the things felt. You become 'crucified' upon the feelings of wealth, freedom and strength. Remain buried in the stillness of these convictions. Then, as a thief in the night and when you least expect it, these qualities will be resurrected in your world as living realities.

———————————~——————————

The worldly minded state of consciousness in all of us which looks into the far distant future and says, "Someday I will reach my goal. Someday I will be happy." This is not the correct attitude, for we must realize that we can take our desire in consciousness . . I AM, Not I will . . now and bring it to birth immediately if only we will believe.

127

It is not stated, "I, Jesus, am the door. I, Jesus AM the way", nor is it said, "Whom do you say that I, Jesus, AM?" It is clearly stated, "I AM the way". The awareness of being is the door through which the manifestations of life pass into the world of form.

Real life is lived in the individuality, the soul, or the real man; and so long as we consciously live in the real man, or in the I AM of being we shall continue to live more and more. We shall thus realize the fullness of life constantly, and constantly grow into a larger measure of that fullness. Life will be full; there will be no lack of life, and no retarded growth in life; in consequence, there will be no evil in life; we shall have perfect freedom and there will be nothing to overcome. Accordingly, we shall fully comply with the great statement, the true way to overcome is to so live that there is nothing to overcome.

This brings us to that much abused statement of the Bible on tithing. Teachers of all kinds have enslaved man with this affair of tithing, for not themselves understanding the nature of tithing and being themselves fearful of lack, they have led their followers to believe that a tenth part of their income should be given to the Lord. Meaning, as they make very clear that, when one gives a tenth part of his income to their particular organization, he is giving his "tenth part" to the Lord . . or is tithing. But remember, "I AM the Lord". Your awareness of being is the God that you give to and you ever give in this manner. Therefore, when you claim yourself to be anything, you have given that claim or quality to God. And your awareness of being, which is no respecter of persons, will return to you pressed down, shaken together, and running over with that quality or attribute which you claim for yourself. Awareness of being is nothing that you could ever name. To claim God to be rich, to be great, to be love, to be all wise, is to define that which cannot be defined. For God is nothing that could ever be named. Tithing is necessary and you do tithe with God. But from now on give to the only God and see to it that you give him the quality that you desire as man to express by claiming yourself to be the great, the wealthy, the loving, the all wise.

The Power of "I AM"

"I AM the Lord, and there is no God beside me," declares my consciousness to be the one and only Lord and beside my consciousness there is no God. "Be still and know that I AM God," means that I should still the mind and know that consciousness is God, "Thou shalt not take the name of the Lord thy God in vain." "I AM the Lord: that is my name." Now that you have discovered your I AM, your consciousness to be God, do not claim anything to be true of yourself that you would not claim to be true of God, for in defining yourself you are defining God.

———————~———————

"I AM the Lord, and there is none else, there is no God beside Me". You, the reader, are the one and only being there is. When you say "I AM," that means the sum total of all the personalities in the world. All other conceptions are projections in space of the one being, yourself. In the Bible, which is a text book on psychology . . metaphysics and man's moods and feelings . . the "I AM" is constantly referred to as, "I AM the way, the truth, and the life". "I AM the Resurrection and the Life". "I AM That I AM". These and similar sayings shine forth in all their true brilliance when once we see that Jesus, the Christ, was not speaking of Himself personally, but of the principle of Being inherent in all mankind.

The Power of "I AM"

"I AM" comes not to destroy, but to fulfill. "I AM", the awareness within you, destroys nothing but ever fills full the molds or conception one has of one's self. It is impossible for the poor man to find wealth in this world, no matter how he is surrounded with it, until he first claims himself to be wealthy. For signs follow, they do not precede. To constantly kick and complain against the limitations of poverty, while remaining poor in consciousness, is to play the fool's game. Changes cannot take place from that level of consciousness, for life is constantly out picturing all levels. Follow the example of the prodigal son. Realize that you, yourself, brought about this condition of waste and lack and make the decision within yourself to rise to a higher level, where the fatted calf, the ring and the robe await your claim.

"Thou shalt not take the name of the Lord thy God in vain." "I AM the Lord: that is my name." Now that you have discovered your I AM, your consciousness to be God, do not claim anything to be true of yourself that you would not claim to be true of God, for in defining yourself you are defining God. That which you are conscious of being is that which you have named God. God and man are one.

131

Give soul to every spoken word and you can heal yourself by saying, "I AM Well;" you can emancipate yourself from every adverse condition by saying, "I AM the Freedom of Divine Truth;" and you can cause every atom in your being to thrill with life and power by saying, "I AM the Strength of the Infinite." Give spirit to every thought you think and every condition you picture in the mind will be realized in the body. Every true desire you feel will be fulfilled, and every dream of greater things will positively come true. What you think you can do you will gain the power to do, because every thought that is filled with the spirit is also filled with the limitless power of the spirit. Give inner power to every statement, and whatever you affirm to be true you will cause to come true. The great word is creative, and if the hidden power of this word is in your statement, it will create whatever your statement may affirm. Therefore, select your statements with wisdom, and pray only for that which you know that you want. When you regain the lost word, all your prayers will be answered and all your desires come true. It is therefore advisable to pray for wisdom first, to desire spirituality first, and to seek first the kingdom of God.

The Power of "I AM"

"I AM the Lord thy God, which has brought thee out of the land of Egypt, out of the house of bondage; thou shalt have not other gods before Me". What a glorious revelation, your awareness now revealed as the Lord thy God! Come, awake from your dream of being imprisoned. Realize that the earth is yours, "and the fullness thereof; the world and all that dwells therein". You have become so enmeshed in the belief that you are man, that you have forgotten the glorious being that you are. Now, with your memory restored, DECREE the unseen to appear and it SHALL appear, for all things are compelled to respond to the Voice of God, Your awareness of being . . the world is AT YOUR COMMAND!

──────────〜────────────

The most difficult thing for man to really grasp is this: That the "I AMness" in himself is God. It is his true being or father state, the only state he can be sure of. The son, his conception of himself, is an illusion. He always knows that he is, but that which he is, is an illusion created by himself . . the father . . in an attempt at self definition.

By the right use of thought we never permit ourselves to say that we cannot. On the contrary we continue to believe and say, "I can do whatever I undertake to do and I AM equal to every occasion." This is our firm conviction when we have come to that place where we really know what is in us, and it is a conviction that is based upon actual scientific fact. Unlimited possibilities are latent in every mind; therefore man is inherently equal to every occasion and he should claim his whole power at all times. If he does not make himself equal to every occasion the cause is that he fails to express all that is in him. But the greater capacity that is within anyone cannot fully express itself so long as thought is created in the likeness of weakness, doubt and limitations. Therefore the right and scientific use of thought becomes the direct channel through which the greatness that is within man may come forth and act in real life.

The Great "I AM." . . Revealed to Moses as the One and Only Real Mind or Power in the Universe. That beside Which there is no other. I AM is another way of saying God. The "I AM" in man is the Life of man; without this "I AM," man could not be.

The Power of "I AM"

The question arises: What is God? God is man's consciousness, his awareness, his I AMness. The drama of life is a psychological one in which we bring circumstances to pass by our attitudes rather than by our acts. The cornerstone on which all things are based is mans concept of himself. He acts as he does, and has the experiences that he does, because his concept of himself is what it is, and for no other reason. Had he a different concept of himself, he would act differently and have different experiences. Man, by assuming the feeling of his wish fulfilled, alters his future in harmony with his assumption, for, assumptions though false, if sustained, will harden into fact. The undisciplined mind finds it difficult to assume a state which is denied by the senses. But the ancient teachers discovered that sleep, or a state akin to sleep, aided man in making his assumption.

There is a rest after every creative process (this is referred to as the seven years) and as we continue creating and generating greater values in life, we go from glory to glory. "And there was neither hammer nor ax, nor any tool of iron heard in the house while it was in building." We create only in the silence. We must learn the effortless way of life which is to "Be still and know that I AM God." If we accept all our desires in consciousness by actually feeling the reality of the wish fulfilled, the objective manifestation of each desire will appear on the screen of space without our devising ways and means. Universal principles always set in motion methods of attainment.

———————— ～～ ————————

If I can feel that I AM That which but a few seconds ago I knew I was not, but desired to be, then I AM no longer hungry to be it. I AM no longer thirsty because I feel satisfied in that state. Then something shrinks within me, not physically but in my feeling, in my consciousness, for that is the creativeness of man. He so shrinks in desire, he loses the desire to continue in this meditation. He does not halt physically, he simply has no desire to continue the meditative act.

The Power of "I AM"

I must contemplate my objective in such a manner that I get the reaction that satisfies. If I do not get the reaction that pleases then Jericho is not seen, for Jericho is a fragrant odor. When I feel that I AM what I want to be I cannot suppress the joy that comes with that feeling. I must always contemplate my objective until I get the feeling of satisfaction personified as Jericho. Then I do nothing to make it visible in my world; for the hills of Gilead, meaning men, women, children, the whole vast world round about me, come bearing witness. They come to testify that I AM what I have assumed myself to be, and AM sustaining within myself. When my world conforms to my assumption the prophecy is fulfilled.

The Power of "I AM"

The only begotten son of God that is within all, within everything, that is the ruling power in every soul, the Supreme I AM in every soul, is never asleep. The statement that the Christ was asleep in the ship is metaphorical. It is not the Christ that is asleep, but our own consciousness of the Christ. When our own consciousness of the Christ is asleep we are not aware of his presence, and he seems to be asleep to us. When we are not aware of this great spiritual power within us, we are unconscious of that power; we are asleep, so to speak, as far as the existence of that power is concerned, and therefore will never think of awakening that power. But when we have attained sufficient spiritual discernment to know the power of the spirit in our own soul, we shall begin to call forth that power. From that moment higher power will be with us, and we shall no longer be victims of the tempest tossed sea; whenever the billows begin to toss or the storms begin to rage, we may call forth the Christ; he will always be with us, and will always respond to the call; he will answer our prayer with his own presence, and in his presence all is beautiful and still.

The Power of "I AM"

If you begin to think that because the earth is moving on its axis every twenty four hours bringing in day and night, and things are going to be better, you will remain confused. God is here now; the very Presence and Life of you. When you say, "I AM" that is God. We do not speak of God to come. God is here already . . your own I AMness . . the Eternal Now. Accept your good now; unite with your desire in consciousness. Enter into the finished state of accomplishment. Let your psychological time clock be, "It is done!" "It is finished!"

All through history, back to the days of Babylon and Egypt, people have been led to believe that they needed an intermediary to approach God, and the Pharisees and the priesthood of Jesus' time tried to do the same thing. However, Moses was instructed to tell the people that God dwells among His people, that the Word of Power is in their mouths and hearts . . I AM. That does not mean that someone else cannot pray for you or give you spiritual help. It means that you can and should go to God direct. Every time you say, "I AM," you are using the power of God to bring certain things into your life, and what you bring will depend upon how you use the I AM and what you attach to it.

The Power of "I AM"

When you say, "I AM," the natural question is, "I AM what?" It has to be qualified, and when you qualify it, you limit it. If you say, "I AM a man," that means you are not a woman. "I AM an American" means you are not a Frenchman or a Spaniard. When you complete the I AM, you limit the expression in one way or another. But God is unlimited, I AM That I AM, unexpressed, creative power, Divine Mind waiting for expression. God has to be expressed, and Man is God in expression. I AM That I AM becomes I AM. Therefore Moses is told, "Thus shalt thou say unto the children of Israel, I AM hath sent me unto you." Man is one with God, the self livingness of God, and thus he has the power to attach the I AM to all the attributes of God: freedom, joy, health, success, abundance. Always I AM connects you with Divine Power because you are the I AM of the I AM That I AM. I AM is the Word of Power. It is the presence of God in you. It insures that you can go direct to God, that you do not need any intermediary.

"I AM the beginning and the end" reveals my consciousness as the cause of the birth and death of all expression.

———————～————————

"I AM the vine and ye are the branches". Consciousness is the 'vine' and those qualities which you are now conscious of being are as 'branches' that you feed and keep alive. Just as a branch has no life except it be rooted in the vine, so likewise things have no life except you be conscious of them. Just as a branch withers and dies if the sap of the vine ceases to flow towards it, so do things in your world pass away if you take your attention from them, because your attention is as the sap of life that keeps alive and sustains the things of your world. To dissolve a problem that now seems so real to you, all that you do is remove your attention from it. In spite of its seeming reality, turn from it in consciousness. Become indifferent and begin to feel yourself to be that which would be the solution of the problem.

By declaring our senses to be spiritual and by speaking the increasing word of the I AM to every one of them, we multiply their capacities and give them a sustaining vigor and vitality. This is done through the simple word of the I AM, backed up by the realization of its spiritual power.

———————～———————

This silent partner in all of us is all wise. You can call It God, if you like, or the Superconscious, the I AM, the Christ within, subconscious wisdom and intelligence or the Higher Self. The point is that this power and wisdom is within each of us, and it is our God given privilege to contact this Super Intelligence and apply It. The Bible says, Acquaint now thyself with him, and be at peace.

The Power of "I AM"

Again, Moses stated, "I AM That I AM". Now here is something to always bear in mind. You cannot put new wine in old bottles or new patches upon old garments. That is, you cannot take with you into the new consciousness any part of the old man. All of your present beliefs, fears and limitations are weights that bind you to your present level of consciousness. If you would transcend this level, you must leave behind all that is now your present self, or conception of yourself. To do this, you take your attention away from all that is now your problem or limitation and dwell upon just being. That is, you say silently but feeling to yourself, "I AM".

Do not condition this 'awareness' as yet. Just declare yourself to be, and continue to do so, until you are lost in the feeling of just being . . faceless and formless. When this expansion of consciousness is attained, then, within this formless deep of yourself give form to the new conception by FEELING yourself to be THAT which you desire to be. You will find within this deep of yourself all things to be divinely possible. Everything in the world which you can conceive of being is to you, within this present formless awareness, a most natural attainment.

"Two shall agree as touching anything and it shall be established on earth".

This agreement is never made between two persons. It is between the awareness and the thing desired. You are now conscious of being, so you are actually saying to yourself, without using words, "I AM". Now, if it is a state of health that you are desirous of attaining, before you have any evidence of health in your world, you begin to FEEL yourself to be healthy. And the very second the feeling "I AM healthy" is attained, the two have agreed. That is, I AM and health have agreed to be one and this agreement ever results in the birth of a child which is the thing agreed upon . . in this case, health. And because I made the agreement, I express the thing agreed. So you can see why Moses stated, "I AM hath sent me". For what being, other than I AM, could send you into expression? None . . for "I AM the way . . Beside me there is no other".

The Power of "I AM"

Moses reflected this general secrecy concerning names and about the Great Name in particular when he asked, "When I come unto the children of Israel, and shall say unto them, The God of your fathers hath sent me unto you; and they shall say to me, What is his name? what shall I say unto them? And God said unto Moses, I AM That I AM. It is a statement that has puzzled religious people down through the ages. In this tremendous statement we find the complete name of God. God is unconditioned being, incorporeal, without beginning or end, the eternal, ever ready, ever present help. Jesus further develops the idea when he says, "God is a Spirit: and they that worship him must worship him in spirit and in truth." I AM That I AM is the complete and final name of God. Any other statement would limit Him in some way. So we begin to see that to know that name gives man power because it identifies the true nature of God. The more we understand the true nature of God the more we will understand our own natures and the power we possess. For make no mistake, there is power in your name when you know how to use it.

Your I AM neither expands nor contracts; nothing alters or adds to it. Before any defined state was, IT is. When all states cease to be, IT is. All defined states or conceptions of yourself are but ephemeral expressions of your eternal being. To be impressed is to be I'm-pressed (I AM pressed . . first person . . present tense). All expressions are the result of I'm-pressions. Only as you claim yourself to be that which you desire to be will you express such desires. Let all desires become impressions of qualities that are, not of qualities that will be. I'm (your awareness) is God and God is the fullness of all, the Eternal NOW, I AM. Take no thought of tomorrow; tomorrow's expressions are determined by today's impressions.

———————————〜〜———————————

If man affirms his unity with the life, substance, and intelligence of God, I AM One with life, I AM One with Substance, I AM One with the intelligence of God, he lays hold of these spiritual qualities.

146

The Power of "I AM"

"I AM the resurrection and the life" is a statement of fact concerning my consciousness, for my consciousness resurrects or makes visibly alive that which I AM conscious of being.

Some of the magic of BEING "the Way" instead of trying to demonstrate an outside force, is shown in the movements of Jesus . . when "instantly he was on the other side of the lake" . . can you think that out . . or make a way by which this would be possible? I believe not . . you have to BE the WAY . . or can you imagine demonstrating the way through a crowd? Unless you discover this wonderful capacity something or somebody is continually blocking your progress . . but once you recognize it . . then you manifest it. You are the Spinner in the Sun. It is wonderful . . "I AM the WAY, the TRUTH and the LIGHT." Your way is within you, chart your own Sky Lanes.

It is recorded that He gave His life that you might live, "I AM come that you might have life and that you might have it more abundantly". Consciousness slays itself by detaching itself from that which it is conscious of being so that it may live to that which it desires to be.

———————⌒⌒———————

Spiritual Marriage . . Spiritually, marriage represents the union of two dominant states of consciousness. When we open the door of the mind by consciously affirming the presence and power of the divine I AM in our midst, there is a marriage or union of the higher forces in being with the lower and we find that we are quickened in every part; the life of the I AM has been poured out for us.

The Power of "I AM"

Jesus saith unto him, I AM the way, and the truth, and the life; no one cometh unto the Father but by me. The great statements of Jesus Christ were never spoken from the personal, but always from the impersonal. No truth ever sprung from the personal mind because it is only the impersonal that can touch the universal, and it is only in the universal that absolute truth can be found. When the mind enters the impersonal state, consciousness comes in touch with the cosmic state of being, and in that state we realize the "I AM" of being. We discern what the "I AM" actually is, and we find that the consciousness of the "I AM is the open door to the limitless vastness of the spiritual universe. "I AM the door." Enter through the door of "I AM" and we pass into that immense world that is found on the upper side, or the divine side of sublime existence.

———————————

One's mental attitude, thoughts, and words are the creative or destructive influences in one's world. Do not say: "I AM sick," "I AM poor," "I AM unhappy." Say: "I AM well," "I AM at peace," "I AM wealthy."

I AM and THAT . . consciousness and that which you are
conscious of being . . have joined and are one; I AM now
nailed or fixed in the belief that I AM this fusion. Jesus or I
AM is nailed upon the cross of that. The nail that binds you
upon the cross is the nail of feeling. The mystical union is
now consummated and the result will be the birth of a child
or the resurrection of a son bearing witness of his Father.
Consciousness is united to that which it is conscious of
being. The world of expression is the child confirming this
union. The day you cease to be conscious of being that which
you are now conscious of being, that day your child or
expression shall die and return to the bosom of his father,
the faceless, formless awareness.

The Power of "I AM"

When sickness appears in the body affirm, "I AM well," and know that it is the truth, because you, the real you, the individuality, the real "I AM," always is well. As you affirm this statement think of the absolute wholeness that permeates your being, and keep the mental eye single upon this absolutely perfect state. In this way perfect health becomes your ideal, and all your thinking will become healthful. Every thought you think will accordingly contain the power of health, and as your thought is so will also be the states and conditions of your personality. The statement, "I AM well," however, should not simply be used when sickness appears in the body. It is a statement that every mind should think at all times, because it is the truth about the true being; and the person who always thinks the truth about the true being, will always be as well in body and mind as he is in the perfections of his true being. Live and think constantly the statement, "I AM well" and you always will be well.

The Power of "I AM"

Be still outwardly, and shout for joy within until it has shattered the walls of your prison. Do you see? If you once glimpse the All Presence in the All Now you will begin to see that I AM not only here and there and everywhere, but I AM everything and partake of the nature of everything through this great Oneness. I AM everything and everybody; I AM ALL.

The numberless unrealized hopes and ambitions of man are the seeds which are buried within the consciousness or virgin womb of man. There they remain like the seeds of earth, held in the frozen waste of winter, waiting for the sun to move northward or for man to return to the knowledge of who he is. In returning he moves northward through recognition of his true self by claiming "I AM the light of the world". When man discovers his consciousness or I AM to be God, the savior of his world, he will be as the sun in its northern passage. All hidden urges and ambitions will then be warmed and stimulated into birth by this knowledge of his true self. He will claim that he is that which heretofore he hoped to be. Without the aid of any man, he will define himself as that which he desires to express. He will discover that his I AM is the virgin conceiving without the aid of man, that all conceptions of himself, when felt, and fixed in consciousness, will be embodied easily as living realities in his world.

The Power of "I AM"

"I AM the Son of the Living God." Do you believe this? If so, you are at this instant facing radical change in the outward expression which will be so far above the old concept that you will stand in amazement at the glory of it all.

———————————————

Jehovah . . The I AM, the spiritual man, the image and likeness of Elohim God. In the King James Version of the Bible the Hebrew "Jehovah" has been translated "Lord." Lord means an external ruler. Bible students say that Jehovah means the self existent One, the I AM. Then instead of reading "Lord" we should read I AM. It makes a great difference whether we think of I AM, self existence within, or "Lord," master without. All Scripture shows that Jehovah means just what God told Moses it meant: I AM. "This is my name forever, and this is my memorial unto all generations".

The Power of "I AM"

Spiritual man is I AM; manifest man is I will. I AM is the Jehovah God of Scripture, and I will is the Adam. It is the I AM man that forms and breathes into the I will man the "breath of life." When we are in the realm of the ideal, we are I AM; when we are expressing ideals in thought or in act, we are I will. When the I will gets so absorbed in its realm of expression that it loses sight of the ideal and centers all its attention in the manifest, it is Adam listening to the serpent and hiding from Jehovah God. This breaks the connection between Spirit and manifestation, and man loses that spiritual consciousness which is his under divine law. In this state of mind the real source of supply is cut off, and there is a drawing upon the reserve forces of the organism, the tree of life. It is in this experience that man is described as being driven out of the Garden of Eden, or the paradise of Being.

The priesthoods of the ancient world, and some of the modern ones too, have tried to keep the masses in darkness about the nature and character of God. It has been their aim to make people lean on an organization, while knowledge of the nature of God might make them too independent. Thus the name of God was kept secret because they have felt that spiritual power was summed up in the name of God, I AM That I AM.

154

Consciousness is the result of the I AM expressing life, thought and being, and therefore consciousness acts on a certain plane, or in a certain part, so long as the I AM gives expression to itself upon that plane, or in that part. Consciousness is always active. An inactive consciousness is as impossible as a dark ray of light. When anything is conscious, it must do something, and it continues to do something, either objectively or subjectively, so long as conscious existence continues.

————————————~———————

Consciousness is the way or door through which things appear. He said, "I AM the way" . . not 'I', John Smith, am the way, but "I AM", the awareness of being, is the way through which the thing shall come. The signs always follow. They never precede. Things have no reality other than in consciousness. Therefore, get the consciousness first and the thing is compelled to appear.

The Power of "I AM"

Instead of sympathizing with the beggars of life at the temple's gate, he declared, "Silver and gold have I none (for thee), but such as I have (the consciousness of freedom), give I unto thee". "Stir up the gift within you" ["Wherefore I put thee in remembrance that thou stir up the gift of God, which is in thee". Stop begging and claim yourself to be that which you decide to be. Do this and you too will jump from your crippled world into the world of freedom, singing praises to the Lord, I AM. "Far greater is He that is in you than he that is in the world" ["Ye are of God, little children, and have overcome them: because greater is He that is in you, than he that is in the world". This is the cry of everyone who finds his awareness of being to be God. Your recognition of this fact will automatically cleanse the temple, your consciousness, of the thieves and robbers, restoring to you that dominion over things, which you lost the moment you forgot the command, "Thou shalt have no other God beside ME".

The Power of "I AM"

When man wills, he attempts to make something which does not now exist appear in time and space. Too often we are not aware of that which we are really doing. We unconsciously state that we do not possess the capacities to express. We predicate our desire upon the hope of acquiring the necessary capacities in future time. "I AM not, but I will be". Man does not realize that consciousness is the Father which does the work, so he attempts to express that which he is not conscious of being. Such struggles are doomed to failure; only the present expresses itself. Unless I AM conscious of being that which I seek, I will not find it. God (your awareness, I AM) is the substance and fullness of all. God's will is the recognition of that which is, not of that which will be. Instead of seeing this saying as "Thine will be done", see it as "Thy will is done". The works are finished. The principle by which all things are made visible is eternal.

I AM the lost word which is hidden within your
consciousness, which IS your consciousness veiled over by a
mystification of human senses. In judging from appearances
you have lost true values, and have accepted shadows as
realities. I AM the lost word, the Word before which the doors
of the universe fly open . . doors in the impassible walls of
human obstacles; doors that lead out on highways never
charted by the human sense because of its limitations. Doors
that belong to the palaces of the kings, fly open at my
coming, and the riches of that which is Caesar's are laid
before me . . to take and do with as I like.

The Power of "I AM"

When a sculptor looks at a formless piece of marble he sees, buried within its formless mass, his finished piece of art. The sculptor, instead of making his masterpiece, merely reveals it by removing that part of the marble which hides his conception. The same applies to you. In your formless awareness lies buried all that you will ever conceive yourself to be. The recognition of this truth will transform you from an unskilled laborer who tries to make it so to a great artist who recognizes it to be so. Your claim that you are now that which you want to be will remove the veil of human darkness and reveal your claim perfectly; I AM That. God's will was expressed in the words of the Widow, "It is well". Man's will would have been, "It will be well". To state, "I shall be well", is to say, "I AM ill". God, the Eternal Now, is not mocked by words or vain repetition. God continually personifies that which is. Thus, the resignation of Jesus (who made Himself equal with God) was turning from the recognition of lack (which the future indicates with "I shall be") to the recognition of supply by claiming, "I AM That; it is done; thank You, Father".

159

"Whatsoever ye shall ask of the Father in my name, he may give it you." Whatsoever you ask means whatever you claim or believe as true will come to pass. The name means the naturalness of the state sought or the mental atmosphere of acceptance. If all we had to say was, "In the name of Jesus rise and walk," we would perform miracles. Obviously there is another meaning. Asking in the name of Jesus means feeling the reality of the fulfilled desire in your own consciousness . . I AM.

———————⌇———————

"Fear not for I AM with thee; and through the rivers, they shall not overflow thee; when thou walkest through the fire, thou shall not be burned." Who is That One? It is your own I AMness; It is the Light or Awareness within you which always goes before you whithersoever thou goest. Your dominant mental attitude or atmosphere is going ahead of you all the time, creating the experiences you will encounter.

The Power of "I AM"

The real man is the soul or the individuality the "I AM"; and that part of man is always perfectly well; in fact, cannot possibly be otherwise than well, a statement that can be demonstrated to the scientifically exact. To know that this is true, and to know that you yourself are the real man that something in human nature that is always perfectly well, is to know the truth the truth that makes man free.

———————～——————

To be, and to be well, will become as one in your thought. You will then have discovered through actual conscious experience that individual existence is impossible without perpetual health, and also that that part of you which is life must therefore be perfectly well at all times. As you grow in the consciousness of your own individual "I AM," this truth will become clearer and clearer, until finally every thought you think will be actually permeated with the realization that the real man is well, and that you are the real man.

It is therefore strictly scientific to think of the body as visible mind, and to think of all the organs in the body as being centers of intelligence. And we shall find that when we take this view of the body, the physical system will no longer be a chunk of clay, but will become a more and more highly organized instrument, responding perfectly to every desire of the ruling mind the conscious mind, the "I AM" in man.

Let us follow the example of Jesus who realized, as man, He could do nothing to change His present picture of lack. He closed the door of His senses against His problem and went to His Father, the one to Whom all things are possible. Having denied the evidence of His senses, He claimed Himself to be all that, a moment before, His senses told him He was not. Knowing that consciousness expresses its likeness on earth, He remained in the claimed consciousness until the doors (His senses) opened and confirmed the rulership of the Lord. Remember, I AM is Lord of all. Never again use the will of man which claims, "I will be". Be as resigned as Jesus and claim, "I AM That".

The Power of "I AM"

Moses discovered God to be man's awareness of being,
when he declared these little understood words, "I AM hath
sent me unto you". The awareness of being as God is stated
hundreds of times in the New Testament. To name but a few:
"I AM the shepherd, I AM the door; I AM the resurrection and
the life; I AM the way; I AM the Alpha and Omega; I AM the
beginning and the end"; and again, "Whom do you say that I
AM?"

———————⁓/———————

"Behold, I stand at the door, and knock: if any man hear
My voice, and open the door, I will come in to him, and will
sup with him, and he with Me". Every desire is the savior's
knock at the door. This knock every man hears. Man opens
the door when he claims, "I AM He". See to it that you let
your savior in. Let the thing desired press itself upon you
until you are I'm-pressed with nowness of your savior; then
you utter the cry of victory, "It is finished".

Before you, [who read this book], a new door has opened.
"I AM the door" and at the same time, "Behold I stand at the
door." When you, through the process of recognition, know
that there is such a thing as a Perfect Universe, created and
sustained by God, who found it very good, you will, by
opening the door of your human consciousness, find that I
AM there, ready to enter into expression. The I AM is your
individual expression of the Universal God. And no sooner is
the door opened than you find that the I AM (your own
individual point of consciousness) is the door of every wall, to
every room (new state of consciousness), to everything that
formed a shell about your good and which you termed
problem. Behold! Behold! It is I . . your Real Self. Be not
afraid.

That person who habitually declares, "I AM so sensitive," is simply producing nervousness, "touchiness" and a tendency to ill temper. Such a person is not sowing good seeds in the mind, but is instead filling the mind with autosuggestion of weakness, nervousness and uncontrolled susceptibility. Such a person, by dwelling on the adverse side of sensitiveness, will cause the mind to be continually impressed by everything that is adverse, and will in addition cause the mind to create adverse conditions within itself. When a person suggests to himself that he is sensitive, he intensifies his susceptibility to external conditions, and will consequently be affected almost constantly by those conditions against his will. He will also impress his mind more and more with the belief that he is constantly being affected by external conditions, and will ere long be almost entirely controlled by environment.

Before Abraham, was I AM. This means before any objectification or manifestation of ideals or desires takes place, the unconditioned or formless awareness, I AM, conditions Itself into the image and likeness of your concept or ideal.

———————⌇———————

Your unconditioned consciousness is impersonal; it is no respecter of persons. Without thought or effort, it automatically expresses every impression that is registered upon it. It does not object to any impression that is placed upon it for; although it is capable of receiving and expressing any and all defined states, it remains forever an immaculate and an unlimited potential. Your I AM is the foundation upon which the defined state or conception of yourself rests; but it is not defined by, nor is it dependent on, such defined states for its being.

The Power of "I AM"

Whatever we impress upon the subconscious that we are now, that the subconscious will create for us now; and everything that we affirm with deep feeling will be impressed upon the subconscious. When we make the statement, "I AM well," we impress the subconscious with the idea that we have health now, and the subconscious will respond by giving us more health now. Many minds, however, do not think it consistent to say they are well when they really feel sick, but this seeming contradiction disappears when you know that the real man is well, and that you are the real man. When you impress the subconscious with the truth about the real man the subconscious will respond by giving the personal man those very qualities that are possessed by the real man.

Since the real man is well and since you are the real man, you would simply be speaking the truth about yourself when you say, "I AM well." At the same time you are impressing health upon the subconscious, and the subconscious will respond by expressing health into every part of mind and body.

There is no one that is not all that is, for consciousness, though expressed in an infinite series of levels, is not divisional. There is no real separation or gap in consciousness. I AM cannot be divided. I may conceive myself to be a rich man, a poor man, a beggar man or a thief, but the center of my being remains the same, regardless of the concept I hold of myself. At the center of manifestation, there is only one I AM manifesting in legions of forms or concepts of itself and "I AM That I AM".

My awareness is my Lord and Shepherd. That which I AM aware of being is the sheep that follow me. So good a shepherd is my awareness of being, it has never lost one sheep or thing that I AM aware of being.

"Far greater is he that is in you than he that is in the world". Believe this. Do not continue in blindness, following after the mirage of masters. I assure you your search can end only in disappointment. "If you deny Me (your awareness of being), I shall deny you also". "Thou shalt have no other God beside ME" . "Be still and know that I AM God". "Come prove me and see if I will not open you the windows of Heaven and pour you out a blessing, that there shall not be room enough to receive it". Do you believe that the I AM is able to do this? Then claim ME to be that which you want to see poured out. Claim yourself to be that which you want to be and that you shall be. Not because of masters will I give it unto you, but, because you have recognized ME (yourself) to be that, I will give it unto you for I AM all things to all.

The conceiver and the conception are one, but the conceiver is greater than his conception. Before Abraham, was I AM. Yes, I was aware of being before I became aware of being man, and in that day when I shall cease to be conscious of being man I shall still be conscious of being. The consciousness of being is not dependent upon being anything. It preceded all conceptions of itself and shall be when all conceptions of itself shall cease to be. "I AM the beginning and the end". That is, all things or conceptions of myself begin and end in me, but I, the formless awareness, remain forever.

"I AM" which is first person and present tense. "But while I AM cometh another steppeth down before me." That which steps down before you are the idle thoughts such as fear, doubt, despair, self pity and similar moods. If you banish these evil spirits or moods, Jesus, your own I AMness will speak softly and say "Rise, take up thy bed and walk." Then the healing comes. Meditating on the eternal verities and the inner glory and beauties of the Deity, man feels a movement within him, this is the Divine Light and it is visible as a golden yellow light. Words cannot always define and formulate the things behind the veil; there are of course many mystical experiences which we cannot express with words, the ecstasy of heavenly bliss, of love and happiness. Meditation is that inner communion which works like a thief in the night, silently in man's own soul. This mood cannot be expressed in words or language as it is beyond all formulation into word symbolism. To enter into the Silence, is intercommunion with the Self or Christ within. This is the nearest approach to the invisible.

I AM is the self definition of the absolute, the foundation on which everything rests. I AM is the first cause-substance. I AM is the self definition of God.

———————⌇———————

I AM is that which, amid unnumbered forms, is ever the same. This great discovery of cause reveals that, good or bad, man is actually the arbiter of his own fate, and that it is his concept of himself that determines the world in which he lives . . and his concept of himself is his reactions to life. In other words, if you are experiencing ill health, knowing the truth about cause, you cannot attribute the illness to anything other than to the particular arrangement of the basic cause-substance, an arrangement which was produced by your reactions to life, and is defined by your concept "I AM unwell". This is why you are told "Let the weak man say, 'I AM strong'", for by his assumption, the cause-substance . . I AM . . is rearranged and must, therefore, manifest that which its rearrangement affirms. This principle governs every aspect of your life, be it social, financial, intellectual, or spiritual.

The Power of "I AM"

Man in the darkness of human ignorance sets out on his search for God, aided by the flickering light of human wisdom. As it is revealed to man that his I AM or awareness of being is his savior, the shock is so great, he mentally falls to the ground, for every belief that he has ever entertained tumbles as he realizes that his consciousness is the one and only savior. The knowledge that his I AM is God compels man to let all others go for he finds it impossible to serve two Gods. Man cannot accept his awareness of being as God and at the same time believe in another deity.

Whenever I say "I AM", I AM [is] creating something. Prayer is believing that we have already received that which we ask. When I say, "I AM", I AM attaching my awareness of being to something. Now, you can lie and not believe what you are saying, but you cannot believe something about "I AM" and not create it. We are creating morning, noon, and night by our "I AM" statements. If you say, "I don't feel well" and you believe it, you are perpetuating illness in your life. You must change those statements to "I feel wonderful". We have to pray (say I AM), believing that it is true, and then we will receive.

The feeling that the "I AM" in you is God reveals to you that there is nothing to be afraid of, and that you are one with Omnipotence, Omniscience, and Omnipresence. No one can steal health, peace, joy, or happiness from you. You no longer live with the many "I's" of fear, doubt, and superstition. You now live in the Divine Presence, and in the consciousness of freedom.

———————————〜〜———————————

The world for centuries with its belief in its material gods has discredited the idea that man's consciousness first creates all things mentally; then he sees them materialize. I AM not of the world, means I AM is man's indwelling consciousness, and it has the complete Power to make its own creation without the help of any man. This basic principle will be the foundation of the new mental world which is about to blossom forth.

The Power of "I AM"

When we are convinced beyond a shadow of a doubt that our own I AMness is our Lord and Master, we know no other. We know whatever we attach feelingly to I AM we become; then the cock crows in us because this truth is a new day in our life. It is a symbol of the awakening to God.

———————— ～✓————————

When the Bible records these words of Paul, please remember that in this case "man" means the "I AM," the conscious spiritual part of yourself. "Woman" or "wife" means your soul; chiefly, in our modern terminology, what is called the subconscious. When we read...... let every one of you ... love his wife even as himself," it means that you have to develop your human character and lift it more and more toward the divine. Where it says the wife must reverence her husband, it means you must learn to control the soul or the subjective conditions.

175

Everything depends upon its attitude towards itself; that which it will not affirm as true of itself cannot awaken in its world. That is, your concept of yourself, such as "I AM strong", "I AM secure", "I AM loved", determines the world in which you live. In other words, when you say, "I AM a man, I AM a father, I AM an American", you are not defining different I AM's; you are defining different concepts or arrangements of the one cause-substance . . the one I AM.

We do well to pay heed to the sayings of the great teachers who have taught that all power is in the "I AM," and to accept this teaching by faith in their bare authority rather than not accept it at all; but the more excellent way is to know why they taught thus, and to realize for ourselves this first great law which all the master minds have realized throughout the ages. It is indeed true that the "lost word" is the one most familiar to us, ever in our hearts and on our lips. We have lost, not the word, but the realization of its power. And as the infinite depths of meaning which the words I AM carry with them, open out to us, we begin to realize the stupendous truth that we are ourselves the very power which we seek.

The Power of "I AM"

No man cometh unto the Father, but by me. This means that no manifestation comes to us save our own consciousness draws it. The me referred to is our own I AMness. Your I AMness is the mother and father of all ideas. When Philip says, "Show us the Father," he is calling forth our dominant mood. One cannot see a mood or a feeling. When you actually become aware of the principle of inner causation, you have discovered your God or your Father in Heaven. Having now discovered the Principle of Life, you must begin to use it wisely. Never permit the suggestion of defeat and impotency to inhibit the free flow of this inner life. Whatever you become aware of determines whether you see lack or confusion or whether you see opulence, order, and harmony in your world.

When man sees the Bible as a great psychological drama, with all of its characters and actors as the personified qualities and attributes of his own consciousness, then . . and then only . . will the Bible reveal to him the light of its symbology. This Impersonal principle of life . . I AM . . which made all things is personified as God. This Lord God, creator of heaven and earth, is discovered to be man's awareness of being. If man were less bound by orthodoxy and more intuitively observant, he could not fail to notice in the reading of the Bibles that the awareness of being is revealed hundreds of times throughout this literature.

The Power of "I AM"

I AM the door. The door is the door of our own consciousness. Everything we experience in life comes through our own consciousness. Our states of consciousness represent what we think, feel, believe, and give consent to. Our states of consciousness are always made manifest. Nothing happens on the outside without first happening on the inside. Before we can manifest health, peace, and abundance, we must first possess our desire in consciousness. We must have the feeling of possession inside. I must be before I can have. The ancients said, "To be is to have."

Now I tell you before it come, that, when it comes to pass,
ye may believe that I AM He. You are always predicting what is to come when you pray. You can have a preview of that which is to come by imagining the end in your mind, rejoicing and thrilling in that mental picture until it is completely absorbed in your mentality. When you experience it on the objective plane, you receive that which you first saw in your mind. You had predicted what was to come to pass through your faith and belief. Ye may believe that I AM He. You are what you contemplate and feel as true; therefore you have discovered that your I AM is your savior.

Regardless of what you are aware of being, you can and do express it without effort. Stop looking for the Master to come; he is with you always. "I AM with you always, even unto the end of the world". You will from time to time know yourself to be many things, but you need not be anything to know that you are. You can, if you so desire, disentangle yourself from the body you wear; in so doing, you realize that you are a faceless, formless awareness and not dependent on the form you are in your expression. You will know that you are; you will also discover that this knowing that you are is God, the Father, which preceded all that you ever knew yourself to be. Before the world was, you were aware of being and so you were saying "I AM", and I AM will be, after all that you know yourself to be shall cease to be.

The Power of "I AM"

The power conceiving itself to be man is greater than its conception. All conceptions are limitations of the conceiver. "Before Abraham, was I AM". Before the world was, I AM. Consciousness precedes all manifestations and is the prop upon which all manifestation rests. To remove the manifestations, all that is required of you, the conceiver, is to take your attention away from the conception. Instead of "Out of sight, out of mind", it really is "Out of mind, out of sight". The manifestation will remain in sight only as long as it takes the force with which the conceiver . . I AM . . originally endowed it to spend itself. This applies to all creation from the infinitesimally small electron to the infinitely great universe. "Be still and know that I AM God".

It is the polarization of Spirit from the universal into the particular, carrying with it all its inherent powers, just as the smallest flame has all the qualities of fire. The I AM in the individual is none other than the I AM in the universal. It is the same Power working in the smaller sphere of which the individual is the center. This is the great truth which the ancients set forth under the figure of the Macrocosm and the Microcosm, the lesser I AM reproducing the precise image of the greater, and of which the Bible tells us when it speaks of man as the image of God.

The Power of "I AM"

Begin now to identify yourself with this presence, your awareness, as the only reality. All manifestations but appear to be; you as man have no reality other than that which your eternal self, I AM, believes itself to be.

———————～———————

The actions of others toward you bear witness to your state of consciousness. If the fruit of the tree is rotten, there is something wrong with the tree; likewise if you are experiencing lack and limitation, you must change the vine. I AM is the vine. You must go within and change your consciousness, and as you change your mental attitude and estimate of yourself, you change your experiences, conditions, and events. There is no one to change but yourself!

"I AM the door". "I AM the way". "I AM the resurrection and the life". "No man (or manifestation) cometh unto My Father save by Me" . . "I AM the way, the truth, and the life: no man cometh unto the Father, but by Me". The I AM (your consciousness) is the only door through which anything can pass into your world. Stop looking for signs. Signs follow; they do not precede. Begin to reverse the statement, "Seeing is believing", to "Believing is seeing". Start now to believe, not with the wavering confidence based on deceptive external evidence but with an undaunted confidence based on the immutable law that you can be that which you desire to be. You will find that you are not a victim of fate but a victim of faith (your own).

———————————~——————————

Only through one door can that which you seek pass into the world of manifestation. "I AM the door". Your consciousness is the door, so you must become conscious of being and having that which you desire to be and to have. Any attempt to realize your desires in ways other than through the door of consciousness makes you a thief and a robber unto yourself.

The Power of "I AM"

Many people are offended by the truth. When you tell them that when they say, "I AM . .that is God" . . they are shocked. They have God away up in the skies, an anthropomorphic being who will judge them on the last day. People are constantly slaying or killing the truth of being. When you hate, resent, quarrel, or become fearful, you are killing love, peace, health, and happiness. You should slay ignorance, fear, and superstition. These false concepts should die and be slain by the sword of truth and illumined reason. If you fear danger, failure, disease, old age, and misfortune, you are murdering . . i.e., psychologically you are separating yourself from God's Love, Light, Truth, and Beauty. We must light the lamp in our synagogue (our mind) and keep it burning with zeal and enthusiasm.

If I be lifted up in consciousness to the naturalness of my desire, I shall automatically draw the manifestation unto me. Consciousness is the door through which life reveals itself. Consciousness is always objectifying itself. To be conscious of being or possessing anything is to be or have that which you are conscious of being or possessing. Therefore, lift yourself to the consciousness of your desire and you will see it automatically out picture itself. To do this, you must deny your present identity. "Let him deny himself". You deny a thing by taking your attention away from it. To drop a thing, problem or ego from consciousness, you dwell upon God . . God being I AM.

(27) **"He it is, who coming after me** is preferred before me, whose shoe's latchet I AM not worthy to unloose".

In verse twenty-seven we are told that the conscious mind is not worthy to unloose the latchet of the shoes of the deeper mind or subjective self. By the subjective self I mean not just the subconscious mind, but the Presence of God or the I AM within us. Feet symbolize understanding, and the shoes cover the feet. In other words, the conscious mind does not know the secret of creation or the manner in which the Infinite Wisdom and Intelligence within man brings things to pass. Its ways are past finding out. The conscious mind cannot unlock or reveal how, when, where, or through what source the answer to prayer will come. Many things seem impossible to the conscious mind, but to the Invisible Power within man, all things are possible. Canst thou believe? All things are possible to him that believeth.

The Power of "I AM"

Man will one day realize that his unconditioned consciousness or I AM is the Virgin Mary desiring to express, that through this law of self-expression he defines himself as that which he desires to express and that without the help or cooperation of anyone he will express that which he has consciously claimed and defined himself as being.

Believe, feel that I AM; know that this knowing one within you, your awareness of being, is God. Close your eyes and feel yourself to be faceless, formless and without figure. Approach this stillness as though it were the easiest thing in the world to accomplish. This attitude will assure your success. When all thought of problem or self is dropped from consciousness because you are now absorbed or lost in the feeling of just being I AM, then begin in this formless state to feel yourself to be that which you desire to be, "I AM That I AM".

There is only One Creative Power. There is only One Source. God is called Awareness, Unconditioned Consciousness, Life. There is only one Life and all things in the world are made inside and out of Life or Consciousness. The Bible calls God I AM, which means Being or Existence. I AM conceives itself to be sun, moon, stars, planets, etc. In fact, everything you see is the I AM in infinite differentiation. There is only one Cause, one Substance, one Source.

Whatever you affix to I AM through feeling, you create in your world of expression. That is what the Bible means when it says that there is nothing made that is not made that way. Nothing is made without feeling. If you feel poor, you become poor; if you feel prosperous, you become prosperous; if you feel dignified, you become dignified.

"Leave all and follow Me" is a double invitation to you.

First, it invites you to turn completely away from all problems and, then, it calls upon you to continue walking in the claim that you are that which you desire to be. Do not be a Lot's wife who looks back and becomes salted or preserved in the dead past. Be a Lot who does not look back but who keeps his vision focused upon the promised land, the thing desired. Do this and you will know that you have found the master, the Master Magician, making the unseen the seen through the command, "I AM That".

———————— ⌇ ————————

Jesus means God is your deliverer, the I AM within you, which receives the impress of your conviction and responds accordingly.

Become Jesus; i.e., become awakened to the Truth and know that there is but one Primal Cause which is your own Consciousness; cease making secondary Causes. To know that your I AM is the only Power, the only Cause, the only Substance, is to free you from all the false gods of the world, enabling you to go forth with the song of God in your heart.

187

Light means Intelligence, in the Bible. Infinite Intelligence is within you (I AM). Feel and know that you are Divinely led in all your ways and that is exactly what you will experience; then you will know and feel the meaning of and the life was the light of men.

I am sure that you are very familiar with the fact that no one can say I AM for you. That statement is in the first person, present tense. It means you are announcing the Presence of God within as Cause and Creator. Notice when you speak to your sister or son you say, "You are." When you speak in the third person you say, "They are."

"I possess the power to say "I AM." No one can say it for me. I now believe I AM what I wish to be. I live, move, and have my being in that mental atmosphere and no person, place, or thing can get in before me or prevent me from being what I long to be; for, according to my belief, is it done unto me.

The Power of "I AM"

There is only one door through which that which you seek can enter your world. "I AM the door". When you say, "I AM", you are declaring yourself to be, first person, present tense; there is no future. To know that I AM is to be conscious of being. Consciousness is the only door. Unless you are conscious of being that which you seek, you seek in vain. If you judge after appearances, you will continue to be enslaved by the evidence of your senses.

———————～～—————————

Unless man discovers that his consciousness is the cause of every expression of his life, he will continue seeking the cause of his confusion in the world of effects, and so shall die in his fruitless search. "I AM the vine and ye are the branches". Consciousness is the vine and that which you are conscious of being is as branches that you feed and keep alive. Just as a branch has no life except it be rooted in the vine, likewise things have no life except you be conscious of them. Just as a branch withers and dies if the sap of the vine ceases to flow towards it, so do things and qualities pass away if you take your attention from them; because your attention is the sap of life which sustains the expression of your life.

189

The Power of "I AM"

The Bible, in Exodus 20:5, says: . . "For I the Lord thy God AM a jealous God" . . This means that you must recognize the Living Spirit Almighty as supreme and omnipotent and refuse to give power to any created thing. In other words, you should not worship a created thing; you must give all allegiance, loyalty and devotion to the One Presence and Power within you, called I AM, or Spirit.

For example, if you are looking for promotion or advancement and you say to yourself: "The boss is blocking my good; but for him I would be promoted and receive greater emoluments," at that moment you have exalted him, a false god. Actually, you are making the boss a god and denying the One Source from Whom all blessings flow. Your subconscious mind knows that your loyalty is divided and consequently does not respond.

You are like the double minded man, unstable in all your ways. On the one hand he is affirming that God is the Source of his supply, meeting all his needs, and then in the next breath he is resenting his employer for not promoting him and increasing his salary. You must never give power to any person, place or thing, for actually you are transferring the power within you to externals. You must give exclusive devotion and loyalty to the One Power within you, Which responds according to the nature of your thoughts and belief.

All that is required of you is to believe. Believe your desires to be garments your savior wears. Your belief that you are now that which you desire to be is proof of your acceptance of life's gifts. You have opened the door for your Lord, clothed in your desire, to enter the moment you establish this belief. "When ye pray, believe that ye have received and it shall be so". "All things are possible to him who believes". Make the impossible possible through your belief; and the impossible (to others) will embody itself in your world. All men have had proof of the power of faith. The faith that moves mountains is faith in yourself. No man has faith in God who lacks confidence in himself. Your faith in God is measured by your confidence in yourself. "I and My Father are one", man and his God are one, consciousness and manifestation are one.

Repeat quietly but with feeling, "I AM . . I AM", until you have lost all consciousness of the world and know yourself just as being. Awareness, the knowing that you are, is Almighty God; I AM.

Do you say to the ideal or desire murmuring in your heart that I AM too old; I do not have enough money; I do not know the right people? Do you say, for example, that due to conditions, inflation, the present administration, events, or circumstances, it is impossible for me to realize my objective? If this is so, you are not disciplining Peter, but you are actually robbing yourself of the joy of experiencing your ideal. The faculty of faith (Peter) knows no obstacles, and recognizes no master or Lord, except his own I AMness. Do you pray for a little while; then give up, and say, "I tried it, but it does not work." If you do, you must begin now to call Peter to discipleship, and you will realize the cherished desire of your heart.

The Power of "I AM"

Consciousness is the way as well as the power which resurrects and expresses all that man will ever be conscious of being. Turn from the blindness of the uninitiated man who attempts to express and possess those qualities and things which he is not conscious of being and possessing; and be as the illumined mystic who decrees on the basis of this changeless law. Consciously claim yourself to be . . I AM . . that which you seek; appropriate the consciousness of that which you see; and you too will know the status of the true mystic, as follows: I became conscious of being it. I AM still conscious of being it. And I shall continue to be conscious of being it until that which I AM conscious of being is perfectly expressed. Yes, I shall decree a thing and it shall come to pass.

In the science of imagination you eliminate all the mental impurities, such as fear, worry, destructive inner talking, self condemnation, and the mental union with other miscellaneous negatives. You must focus all your attention on your ideal, and refuse to be swerved from your purpose or aim in life. As you get mentally absorbed in the reality of your ideal, by loving and remaining faithful to it, you will see your desire take form in your world. In the book of Joshua it says, "Choose ye this day whom ye shall serve." Let your choice be, "I AM going to imagine whatsoever things are lovely and of good report."

The Power of "I AM"

Divine healing is based upon the supposition that we speak from an absolute center . . the I AM or first cause. The treatment is unconditioned by any element of time as the past, present, or future. It is not conditioned by anything that has ever transpired. It would not be possible for a metaphysician or spiritual healer to do effective work, if he judged according to appearances.

He has forgotten his divine origin and accepts the opinion of man as the truth; consequently, he sins or errs because he does not know that his own I AMness is the God that he seeks. He dwells, therefore, in the land of many Gods and the belief in many powers. The man who loves Truth and practices the Presence of God is like a magnetized piece of steel. The man who is asleep to God is like a demagnetized piece of steel . . the magnetic current is there, but it is asleep within him. When we dwell in the presence, the electronic and atomic structure of our body reforms and vibrates accordingly.

The Power of "I AM"

I AM (your awareness of being) is the power resurrecting and making alive that which in your awareness you desire to be. The Bible gives conflicting stories as to what happened to Judas. It is significant that we know that we are not dealing with a man, but we are concerned with a mental attitude of lies, fears, and unholy beliefs. Judas is the personification of the adversary, or our negative thought which comes from the world around us; in other words, Judas is our false belief. Also, Judas is the type of man who believes power and honor are in worldly possessions and supremacy over others. We must die or commit suicide to these false beliefs. Realize that the only peace and the only source of supply and power are from God . . "I AM". We must give complete recognition to Him. "I AM, and there is none else." When we die to the belief in disease, there is only health. When we cease believing the lie, symbolized by Judas, God or good is revealed. This is the reason Judas reveals or betrays Jesus. Jesus symbolizes the solution or the realization of your desire.

The Power of "I AM"

The Door to True Expression

"Verily, verily, I say unto you, He that entereth not by the door into the sheepfold, but climbeth up some other way, the same is a thief and a robber. But he that entereth in by the door is the shepherd of the sheep."

I AM is the door. This means your own consciousness is the door to all expression. In other words, you must have the mental equivalent established in your subconscious mind in order to manifest what you desire and what you want to achieve in life. When you try to accomplish on the outside what you have not felt as true on the inside, you will fail, e.g., when a man claims to be something other than what he really feels himself to be, such as claiming that he is a great actor when in his heart he does not feel it to be true, he is robbing himself and is the thief mentioned in the above verses.

He must claim and honestly feel himself to be the great actor and, further, dramatize the role; and as he continues to claim and feel that he is the great actor, the power of the subconscious will back him up and he will manifest the role. The embodied states of mind are the sheep mentioned. The feeling of being what you long to be must always precede the embodied state, resulting in the manifestation of what is felt as true subjectively.

The Power of "I AM"

"As Moses lifted up the serpent in the wilderness even so must the Son of Man be lifted up". The serpent symbolizes man's present conception of himself as a worm of the dust, living in the wilderness of human confusion. Just as Moses lifted himself from his worm-of-the-dust conception of himself to discover God to be his awareness of being, "I AM hath sent me", so must you be lifted up. The day you claim, as did Moses, "I AM That I AM", that day your claim will blossom in the wilderness. After this is accomplished, define yourself as that which you desire to be by feeling yourself to be the thing desired: I AM That. This understanding that you are the thing desired will cause a thrill to course through your entire being. When the conviction is established and you really believe that you are that which you desired to be, then the second "I AM" is uttered as a cry of victory. This mystical revelation of Moses can be seen as three distinct steps: I AM; I AM free; I really AM!

I AM fixed on high in the spirit of truth

The I AM of every soul can truthfully make this statement, for real being is permanently established in the true life of the spirit, and as every individual is the I AM of his own being, every individual, to speak the truth, must make this statement about himself. To realize the truth of this statement is to enter more and more into the fixed state of true being, and to grow in the realization of this state is to gain that absolute safety and security where the soul finds complete divine protection. To be in the spirit of truth is to be in the very life of true existence, and to be fixed in this life is to occupy a permanent place in God's own beautiful world. In other words, to be fixed in the spirit of truth, is to be anchored in God, and we can readily realize how absolutely secure such a state of being must be.

When we make this statement we should try to realize what existence in the truth must necessarily mean, how it must feel to be in the consciousness of the spirit of such an existence, and what a life must hold in store that is permanently established on the very heights of that existence. The more fully we enter into the soul of the truth that this statement conveys, the sooner we shall realize the truth itself; and when we do, we shall know that we are fixed on high, permanently established in the spirit of truth, forever anchored in God.

———————————~——————————

Live in the conviction that "I AM greater than all my ills or failures; that I AM greater than the limitations of my circumstances, and greater than any condition that I can possibly meet." When you feel that you are greater than your ills, those ills cannot long remain, because what you inwardly feel, you realize, and what you realize, you bring forth into living expression. To open the mind to the great thought that the health that is within you is greater than any disease than you can ever know, is to open your life to the power of that health; and when the greater power of the health that is within you comes forth into the life of every atom in your being, the lesser power of disease, weakness or adverseness must vanish completely. No disease can long remain in your system after you begin to live in the constant conviction that the absolute health that is within you is infinitely greater and more powerful than all the sickness in the world. Nor can failure continue after you begin to realize that you, in the reality of your whole being, have the power to turn the tide of any circumstance that may ever appear in your world. The good that is within you is larger and more powerful than all the troubles, misfortunes or disappointments in existence; and this good, when fully recognized by you, will begin to work for you. It will work for your good, and will turn to good account everything that can happen.

The I AM within you is the Virgin Mary, which is capable of infinite conceptions of Itself without the aid of any man.

The Power of "I AM"

The word virgin in the Bible means a pure mind, or mind dedicated to God. The word Mary comes from "mare," meaning the sea, all of which means the pure stream of consciousness. Maya, the name of the mother of Buddha, has the same meaning. The words Queen of Heaven, Star of the Sea, Isis, Queen Esther, etc., all mean the same thing . . the I AM, or Presence of God in your subconscious depths.

God, or I AM, gives birth to the entire cosmos and all things contained therein and is the only Presence and Power. Actually, all the symbols of Christmas have to deal with the human heart, or your subconscious mind. The star spoken of represents the Infinite Intelligence within you, which guides and directs you and reveals to you the answer.

You can claim that God is guiding you and revealing to you the answer or solution to your problem. Accept the truth that the nature of Infinite Intelligence is to respond to you, and you will receive an answer without the aid of any man. You can boldly affirm, "I AM whole, perfect, strong, loving, illumined, prosperous and inspired." As you continue to affirm these truths and feel and believe what you claim, without the help or cooperation of anyone, you will express what you feel to be true. Remember, whatever you attach to I AM, you become.

The Power of "I AM"

"I AM the vine, ye are the branches". . . A branch is rooted in the vine. In order to change the fruit you must change the vine. I AM is God, Being, Life, Awareness; and seven billion people in the world are rooted in the I AM, or Life Principle. All men and women are extensions of the I AM, or Life Principle; therefore, they are all rooted in you and you in them. Like fruit, others bear witness to the state of consciousness in which you dwell. Your I AMness, your Consciousness, is the way in which you change your world. Whatever you attach to I AM you become. As you affirm with feeling, I AM illumined, inspired, loving, harmonious, peaceful, happy and strong, you will resurrect these qualities that lie dormant within you, and wonders will happen in your life. When men and women help you in the realization of your dreams, they are playing their part and are messengers testifying to your beliefs and convictions. You wrote the play, and other men and women execute the parts conforming to your concept of yourself.

-------------⁓/-------------

Man, not knowing that his world is his individual consciousness out pictured, vainly strives to conform to the opinion of others rather than to conform to the one and only opinion existent, namely, his own judgment of himself. When Jesus discovered His consciousness to be this wonderful law of self government, He declared, "And now I sanctify Myself that they also might be sanctified through the truth" "And for their sakes I sanctify Myself, that they also might be sanctified through the truth", He knew that consciousness was the only reality, that things objectified were nothing more than different states of consciousness. Jesus warned His followers to seek first the Kingdom of Heaven . . that state of consciousness that would produce the thing desired . . and all things would be added to them. He also stated, "I AM the truth". He knew that man's consciousness was the truth or cause of all that man saw his world to be. Jesus realized that the world was made in the likeness of man. He knew that man saw his world to be what it was because man was what he was. In short, man's conception of himself determines that which he sees his world to be.

———————～———————

"To him that hath shall be given, and from him that hath not shall be taken away". You have in manifestation exactly what you have in consciousness (I AM) . . good, bad, or indifferent. Why waste any further time trying to change the outside condition, when it is held in manifestation by the inner state of consciousness? To him that hath shall be given . . because he will take, be it a good, bad, or indifferent manifestation. A man with a consciousness full of troubles always gets more troubles, and he finds them everywhere. It is what he finds to be true, and so he must find it in manifestation. No wonder the prophet asked, "What have you in your house?" What have you in your house, your consciousness? You have just what you conceive the Father within to be, and you cannot increase this until you begin to recognize the nature of the pure substance of Spirit from which all things come into manifestation. Until you recognize the true Self, and stop trying to doctor up an old body or condition, you cannot know the glory of the Son of God. You are not an old creature patched up. You are a new creature in Christ Jesus. You are a new, perfect manifestation; to recognize this is to claim your rights and press your claim by the serene power of the Almighty.

"I AM the Lord and beside Me there is none else". You cannot command that which is not. As there is no other, you must command yourself to be that which you would have appear. Let me clarify what I mean by effective command. You do not repeat like a parrot the statement, "I AM That I AM"; such vain repetition would be both stupid and fruitless. It is not the words that make it effective; it is the consciousness of being the thing which makes it effective. When you say, "I AM", you are declaring yourself to be. The

The Power of "I AM"

word that in the statement, "I AM That I AM", indicates that which you would be. The second "I AM" in the quotation is the cry of victory. This whole drama takes place inwardly with or without the use of words. Be still and know that you are. This stillness is attained by observing the observer. Repeat quietly but with feeling, "I AM . . I AM", until you have lost all consciousness of the world and know yourself just as being. Awareness, the knowing that you are, is Almighty God; I AM. After this is accomplished, define yourself as that which you desire to be by feeling yourself to be the thing desired: I AM That. This understanding that you are the thing desired will cause a thrill to course through your entire being. When the conviction is established and you really believe that you are that which you desired to be, then the second "I AM" is uttered as a cry of victory. This mystical revelation of Moses can be seen as three distinct steps: I AM; I AM free; I really AM!

The Names in the Nativity

Joseph represents your conscious, reasoning mind with its superficial beliefs, opinions, creeds, dogmas, traditions, thoughts and fears . . the five sense man who judges according to appearances. Joseph also means imagination and the autocratic intellect.

205

The Power of "I AM"

Mary represents the subconscious mind, full of wisdom and intelligence, the seat of intuition, memory and emotion. Within your subconscious is the I AM, the Higher Self, sometimes referred to as the Superconscious. Mary is with child of the Holy Ghost . . the Holy Spirit, the Presence of God, and Joseph is instructed to keep away, which means that your conscious mind is not to impregnate and browbeat your subconscious with its false sense knowledge. Joseph is the guardian of the threshold and is to see to it that nothing enters into the subconscious that does not fill the soul with joy. Joseph . . the conscious mind . . should protect the subconscious from all pollution and negative impressions.

Jesus and Joshua are synonymous. Both names mean the same thing; i.e., God is your Savior, or God is the Emancipator. In other words, God within you is the solution to all your problems. The realization of your heart's desire is your savior. For example, if you are in prison, freedom is your savior; if sick, health is your savior; if dying of thirst, water would be your savior; and if lost in the jungle, God, or the Guiding Principle, would lead you out.

The inn is the outer meeting place of superficial human beliefs, fears, customs, traditional concepts, and beliefs of the mass mind. In other words, it is the law of averages, what the mass mind is thinking. When you inform the average man that the Infinite Intelligence within him can heal his body, inspire him, guide him and reveal to him all

206

answers, and that It actually is the Presence of God, he all too frequently rejects it and instead postulates an anthropomorphic being up in the skies who judges, punishes and condemns. There is no room in his mind for the realization that his awareness of the Presence and Power of God and his contact and application of It in his life is his real savior. The stable is the subconscious mind, the place where the "animi" or "animals" (basic urges, feelings, emotions, passions) are to be found waiting for the coming of the Shepherd, the Lord and Master.

The Shepherd is your dominant conviction of God and the truths of life which keep a check on the sheep (the harmonious feelings and ideals) lest the wolves (destructive emotions) eat them up or destroy them. Your thoughts need a shepherd, which means your dominant idea of the goodness and love of God in the land of the living controls all lesser thoughts and emotions, actions and reactions. The nativity, or birth of God, is taking place in you when you begin to radiate light, love, truth and beauty to all those around you and to all people everywhere. Become a channel for Divine love, harmony, peace and joy, and all the Divine forces will hasten to minister to your eternal growth and expansion in the light.

The Power of "I AM"

He Had the Wrong Self Image

In counseling a young man whose basic problem was that he was chronically ill, it became apparent that as soon as he recovered from one ailment he acquired another sickness. He had had six operations in six years. He maintained an image of himself as being sick. He had been told when he was young that he was sickly and would always be weak. He accepted this and, as a result, learned to be unhealthy. His belief that he was always destined to be sickly was in his subconscious mind, and whatever he believed came to pass. Every perfect gift cometh down from the Father of Light, with Whom there is no change, neither shadow of turning. Where is the Father? How long will you look for Him in some far off locality? How long will you seek among the husks for the substance of life? Every gift that is to come to you as John Smith will proceed out of the center of the I AM consciousness within yourself. Behold, I AM He that should come. I AM That I AM has sent me into expression. It is wonderful, it is wonderful. Blessings, blessings, blessings. I AM the Son of the Living God. Claim your rights, and press your claim. Son of the Living God, I salute you! Arise! Leave your human reasoning and go unto your Father within. Let the filthy be filthy still. Let all those who wish to sell the Word of God continue to do so. Let those who what to argue continue their arguments. Let those judges and spiritual busybodies cast their stones. Go thy way; it is well with thee. The new secret has been revealed to you; do you hear?

———————⁓——————

It is written, "My house shall be called of all nations a house of prayer, but ye have made it a den of thieves" ". . .for Mine house shall be called an house of prayer for all people". The thieves who rob you are your own false beliefs. It is your belief in a thing not the thing itself that aids you. There is only one power: I AM He. Because of your belief in external things, you think power into them by transferring the power that you are to the external thing. Realize you yourself are the power you have mistakenly given to outer conditions.

Stop asking yourself whether or not you are worthy or unworthy to claim yourself to be that which you desire to be. You will be condemned by the world only as long as you condemn yourself. You do not need to work out anything. The works are finished. The principle by which all things are made and without which there is not anything made that is made is eternal. You are this principle. Your awareness of being is this everlasting law. You have never expressed anything that you were not aware of being and you never will. Assume the consciousness of that which you desire to express. Claim it until it becomes a natural manifestation. Feel it and live within that feeling until you make it your nature. Here is a simple formula. Take your attention from your present conception of yourself and place it on that ideal of yours, the ideal you had heretofore thought beyond your reach. Claim yourself to be your ideal, not as something that you will be in time, but as that which you are in the immediate present. Do this, and your present world of limitations will disintegrate as your new claim rises like the phoenix from its ashes. "Be not afraid nor dismayed by reason of this great multitude; for the battle is not yours, but God's". You do not fight against your problem; your problem will only live as long as you are conscious of it. Take your attention away from your problem and the multitude of reasons why you cannot achieve your ideal. Concentrate your attention entirely upon the thing desired. "Leave all and follow me". In the face of seemingly mountainous obstacles, claim your freedom. The consciousness of freedom is the Father of freedom. It has a way of expressing itself which no man knows. "Ye shall not need to fight in this battle. Set yourself, stand still, and see the salvation of the Lord with you". "I AM the Lord". I AM (your consciousness) is the Lord. The consciousness that the thing is done, that the work is finished, is the Lord of any situation.

The Power of "I AM"

Instead of looking for new places and new scenes in the without, whenever you feel the need of a change, look for new sensations and experiences in your own consciousness. What exists in the within is just as real as that which exists in the without, and it is of more importance to understand. Therefore, by training the mind to take journeys into the beautiful worlds within, you are not only acquiring the art of forming new mental impressions within; you are also enlarging mind and consciousness. You are gaining valuable information about many things that material man knows nothing of; and you are preparing the way for real freedom and much higher development. The real purpose, however, of these journeys to the within, should be the change of thought, and for that reason should be taken whenever the need of mental change is felt. To begin, realize that the larger life within is the fullness of life, and cannot in any way lack the real essentials of life. Realize that the worlds within are ideal worlds, and are therefore not imperfect in any way. Realize that the new inner states of consciousness that you may discern, contain the unlimited possibilities of absolute existence, and are therefore neither incomplete nor imperfect in any way whatever. Then realize that those inner places are not separated from you, but are necessary parts of your whole being, and also that the I AM, the real you, is at the very center of this whole being; and lastly, realize that whenever you turn your attention upon the potential, the within, the ideal, you are looking upon something that contains within itself all the elements of absolute perfection.

———————⟋⌒⟍⟍———————

Stop trying to change the world since it is only the mirror. Man's attempt to change the world by force is as fruitless as breaking a mirror in the hope of changing his face. Leave the mirror and change your face. Leave the world alone and change your conceptions of yourself. The reflection then will be satisfactory. Freedom or imprisonment, satisfaction or frustration can only be differentiated by the consciousness of being. Regardless of your problem, its duration or its magnitude, careful attention to these instructions will in an amazingly short time eliminate even the memory of the problem. Ask yourself this question: "How would I feel if I were free?" The very moment you sincerely ask this question, the answer comes. No man can tell another the satisfaction of his desire fulfilled. It remains for each within himself to experience the feeling and joy of this automatic change of consciousness. The feeling or thrill that comes to one in response to his self questioning is the Father state of consciousness or Foundation Stone upon which the conscious change is built. Just how this feeling will embody itself no one knows, but it will; the Father (consciousness) has ways that no man knows; it is the unalterable law. All things express their nature. As you wear a feeling, it becomes your nature. It might take a moment or a year . . it is entirely dependent upon the degree of conviction. As doubts vanish and you can feel "I AM This", you begin to develop the fruit or the nature of the thing you are feeling yourself to be.

***

So it is recorded that this Son and Savior of the world was born of a virgin. It is also recorded that this virgin mother was traveling through the night, that she stopped at an inn and was given the only available room among the animals and there in a manger, where the animals fed, the shepherds found the Holy Child. The animals with whom the Holy Virgin was lodged are the holy animals of the zodiac. There in that constantly moving circle of astronomical animals stands the Holy Mother, Virgo, and there you will see her every midnight of December 24th, standing on the eastern horizon as the sun and savior of the world starts his journey northward. Psychologically, this birth takes place in man on that day when man discovers his consciousness to be the sun and savior of his world. When man knows the significance of this mystical statement, "I AM the light of the world", he will realize that his I AM, or consciousness, is the sun of his life, which sun radiates images upon the screen of space. These images are in the likeness of that which he, as man, is conscious of being. Thus qualities and attributes which appear to move upon the screen of his world are really projections of this light from within himself.

"And God said unto Moses, I AM That I AM: and he said, Thus shall thou say unto the children of Israel, I AM hath sent me unto you . . "This is my name forever, and this is my memorial unto all generations." "I AM," then, is God's name. Every time you say, "I AM sick," "I AM weak," "I AM discouraged," are you not speaking God's name in vain, falsely. I AM cannot be sick; I AM cannot be weary, or faint, or powerless; for I AM is All-Life, All-Power, All-Good. "I AM," spoken with a downward tendency, is always false, always "in vain." A commandment says, "Thou shalt not take the name of Jehovah thy God in vain; for Jehovah will not hold him guiltless that taketh his name in vain." And Jesus said, "By thy words thou shalt be justified, and by thy words thou shalt be condemned." If you speak the "I AM" falsely, you will get the result of false speaking. If you say, "I AM sick," you will get sickness; if you say, "I AM poor," you will get poverty; for the law is, "Whatsoever a man soweth, that shall he also reap." "I AM," spoken upward, toward the good, the true, is sure to out picture in visible good, in success, in happiness. Does all this sound foolish to you? Do you doubt that such power goes with the speaking of God's name? If so, just go alone, close your eyes, and in the depth of your own soul say over and over the name "I AM." Soon you will find your whole being filled with a sense of power that you never had before . . power to overcome, power to accomplish, power to do all things.

───────── ⌒⌒ ─────────

And God said, Let Us make man in Our image, after Our likeness. Having discovered God to be our awareness of being and this unconditioned changeless reality (the I AM) to be the only creator, let us see why the Bible records a trinity as the creator of the world. In the 26th verse of the first chapter of Genesis, it is stated, "And God said, Let Us make man in Our image". The churches refer to this plurality of Gods as God the Father, God the Son and God the Holy Spirit. What is meant by "God the Father, God the Son and God the Holy Spirit" they have never attempted to explain for they are in the dark concerning this mystery. The Father, Son and Holy Spirit are three aspects or conditions of the unconditioned awareness of being called God. The consciousness of being precedes the consciousness of being something. That unconditioned awareness which preceded all states of awareness is God . . I AM. The three conditioned aspects or divisions of itself can best be told in this manner: The receptive attitude of mind is that aspect which receives impressions and therefore may be likened to a womb or Mother. That which makes the impression is the male or pressing aspect and is therefore known as Father. The impression in time becomes an expression, which expression is ever the likeness and image of the impression; therefore this objectified aspect is said to be the Son bearing witness of his Father-Mother. An understanding of this mystery of the trinity enables the one who understands it to completely transform his world and fashion it to his own liking.

—————————〜〜————————

When we examine the mind of the average person, we find that they usually identify themselves with mind or body. They either think that they are body or that they are mind, and therefore they can control neither mind nor body. The "I AM" in their nature is submerged in a bundle of ideas, some of which are true and some of which are not, and their thought is usually controlled by those ideas without receiving any direction whatever from that principle within them that alone was intended to give direction. Such a one lives in the lower story of human existence but as we can control life only when we give directions from the upper story, we discover just why the average person neither understands their forces nor has the power to use them. They must first

The Power of "I AM"

elevate themselves to the upper story of the human structure, and the first and most important step to be taken in this direction is to recognize the "I AM" as the ruling principle and that the "I AM" is you. Another method that will be found highly important in this connection is to take a few moments every day and try to feel that you . . the "I AM" . . are not only above mind and body, but in a certain sense, distinct from mind and body; in fact, try to isolate the "I AM" for a few moments every day from the rest of your organized being. This practice will give you what may be termed a perfect consciousness of your own individual "I AM," and as you gain that consciousness you will always think of the supreme "I AM" whenever you think of yourself. Accordingly, all your mental actions will, from that time on, come directly from the "I AM"; and if you will continue to stand above all such actions at all times, you will be able to control them and direct them completely.

In the course of human experience progress for man sometimes seems impossibly difficult, but this is because we are in the thought of limitation, dependent upon material things, and thus subject to "the law of the flesh." However, when we catch the vision of the Cosmic Christ and identify ourselves with that, we no longer come under the law of

217

outer things, but, as Paul said, under grace. No human being ever lived who was more under bondage of law than Paul. He was so steeped in it from his earliest days that he almost lost his faith in God. Then he realized the Truth one day, and hundreds of years later, Luther, reading those wonderful words that Paul wrote, was also set free in the same way: "The just shall live by faith." This means that when you see the vision of the divine possibility within you and stretch forth your hands toward it, you are no longer under the law of sin and bondage. The limitations and weaknesses of your own character, the mistakes of the past, no longer have the slightest power to keep you back. You are under the law of grace. Calvary is past and Easter morning is dawning. It is the dawn of Easter and never again will you have the Thursday or Friday to go through. You are under grace. This is the real law of scientific prayer. It is withdrawing yourself from the limited condition into the spiritual realm where there is freedom and dominion. How do you withdraw yourself? By some physical act? No. It is a matter of attention. When your attention is centered on limitation, on your weaknesses or other people's weaknesses, on your difficulties, your sickness, your fears, you are in bondage to these things. As Paul says, "His servants ye are to whom you obey." But when you lift your attention . . your I AM . . out of the limited things into the spiritual, then you are in a state of consciousness where the limiting things no longer have any power. This is why scientific prayer performs miracles right and left. This is why it turns people's lives upside down, takes them out of beds of pain and sickness, and brings them out of lives of sin and self contempt. Scientific prayer does this . . not now and again, not occasionally, but every day in the week in every quarter of the world. It does it whenever and wherever one raises his consciousness to the presence of God.

Emmet Fox stated previously that God, the I AM That I AM, was differentiated into men and women. I AM is the lost word and secret Name of God in us. It is our true identity; our real name; it is Divine Spirit, which is our real eternal self; it was never born and will never die. Knowing this final name of God, says Fox, is what gives one power, because it identifies one with the true nature of God. He remarks that a statement such as I AM elicits the question, I AM what? This requires a qualification, and when one completes the sentence, one limits it. An answer such as I AM a man means you are not a woman and such qualifications limit the expression in one way or another. However, the qualification of I AM That I AM does not limit any expression. It states the absolute . . God! Fox maintains that God is unlimited, I AM That I AM, unexpressed, creative power, Divine Mind waiting for expression and man is God's expression. It is man's oneness with the divine that empowers a person and allows one to attach the I AM to all the attributes of God (such as freedom, joy, health, success and abundance). I AM always connects one with divine power because we are the I AM of the I AM That I AM. It is the presence of God in you. It insures that you can go direct to God, that you do not need any intermediary. This last statement relates well to an earlier observation in which Wilber distinguishes between the God of the subtle realm with whom one can bargain for one's salvation, and the God of the causal realm where all communication is transcended, for one actually becomes that oneness.

I AM is your true identity. I AM is your real name, and in that name there is power. I AM is Divine Spirit, your real eternal self. It was never born and will never die. I AM is never sad, never grows old, never worries or sins or knows fear. However, this I AM is filtered through your consciousness and so you have the power of misusing it, as many people do. You have free will and the power to choose whether you will use it constructively or destructively. You can attach the I AM to your true nature and experience great power, or you can misuse it by misrepresenting yourself in many limited ways.

The Power of "I AM"

You are constantly drawing to yourself that which you are conscious of being. Change your conception of yourself from that of the slave to that of Christ. Don't be embarrassed to make this claim; only as you claim, "I AM Christ", will you do the works of Christ.

My consciousness is the Father who draws the manifestation of life to me. The nature of the manifestation is determined by the state of consciousness in which I dwell. I AM always drawing into my world that which I AM conscious of being.

To accomplish this seemingly impossible feat, you take your attention away from your problem and place it upon just being. You say silently but feelingly, "I AM". Do not condition this awareness but continue declaring quietly, "I AM . . I AM". Simply feel that you are faceless and formless and continue doing so until you feel yourself floating. "Floating" is a psychological state which completely denies the physical.

Through practice in relaxation and willfully refusing to react to sensory impressions, it is possible to develop a state of consciousness of pure receptivity. It is a surprisingly easy accomplishment. In this state of complete detachment, a definite singleness of purposeful thought can be indelibly engraved upon your unmodified consciousness. This state of consciousness is necessary for true meditation. This wonderful experience of rising and floating is the signal that you are absent from the body or problem and are now present with the Lord; in this expanded state you are not conscious of being anything but I AM . . I AM; you are only conscious of being.

When this expansion of consciousness is attained, within this formless deep of yourself, give form to the new conception by claiming and feeling yourself to be that which you, before you entered into this state, desired to be. You will find that within this formless deep of yourself all things appear to be divinely possible. Anything that you sincerely feel yourself to be while in this expanded state becomes, in time, your natural expression. And God said, "Let there be a firmament in the midst of the waters". Yes, let there be a firmness or conviction in the midst of this expanded consciousness by knowing and feeling I AM That, the thing desired.

———————~———————

The earth is the Lord's, and the fullness thereof; the world, and they that dwell therein.

These words are constantly quoted on all sorts of occasions, but the context in which they are used seldom gives evidence of any spiritual understanding of their true import. At worst, I have seen them used as an attempt at consolation in the face of death or of great financial misfortune. The implication seems to be that as everything belongs to God, He is entitled to destroy whatever He pleases without consulting the feelings of mankind. At best, they are taken in the sense of pious, but rather vague, recognition of God as the general source of our supply. Of course, even the vaguest recognition of this primary fact is better than no recognition at all; but unless we get a definite, scientific understanding of the meaning underlying the words, we shall derive no real profit from them.

To suppose that God, the Great Source, Substance Itself, could cause, or even endorse death or misfortune, is the deadly error that lies at the root of all our troubles; and it is characteristic of the carnal mind thus to pervert a text which, above most others in the Bible, explains the real Law of Life and Prosperity. This carnal mind, as St. Paul calls it, is, of course, nothing but our own restricted and ignorant manner of thinking. To be ignorant of the laws of life, or to misunderstand them, cannot, it is true, change those laws; but it can and does cause us suffering and deprivation of every kind . . even to the death belief itself . . until such habits of thought are corrected.

The key to the true meaning of this first stanza is found in the two pivotal words, "Lord" and "earth," and here at the very beginning we must pause and ask ourselves what we mean by the Lord. "God, of course," we will say, and that is true; but in the Bible the word "Lord," as a rule, means God in the special sense of our own Indwelling Christ; our own true identity, the Divine Spark . . the I AM. So this verse states, once and for all, that the "earth" which, as we know, is a general term covering all our expression or manifestation, is under the jurisdiction of the I AM. Now all trouble of every kind really arises from the belief that the "earth" is subject to the dominion of some outer power or law which is able to govern it independently of the I AM, or to destroy it altogether. But the Law of Being is, that man is the image and likeness of God, and has full dominion over all his conditions . . all of them . . and our Psalm emphasizes this wonderful fact by adding the world and they that dwell therein. Our earth, which is our world, down to every detail of our lives, is really under our own dominion, and is made and unmade by our word.

---

(6) Jesus saith unto him, I AM the way, the truth and the life; no man cometh unto the father but by me.

Verse six does not refer to a man. It means man's inner consciousness is the way to health, freedom, and peace of mind. Your I AMness is the door to all manifestations and expressions. You become what you contemplate. Your consciousness or awareness is the truth because whatever you feel as true will come to pass. The realization of your desire would free you this moment if you were sick or in prison. This would be the truth that would set you free.

You can make a test for yourself. Begin to believe that life is harmonious and friendly and people are wonderful. You will find life will take on a new meaning because of your new attitude. It is done unto you as you believe. You are operating a law of your own mind. You have discovered a truth which sets you free from despondency, gloom, and loneliness. When you believe the world is good, you discover life corresponds to your attitude and your world becomes good. To know that your thoughts and feelings direct your destiny enables you to soar aloft above the problems of the world and dwell on the solution in the realm of spirit and mind. You know that wherever your consciousness is, there will your body be also. Your feet and hands will go where your consciousness is. If you say, "I AM poor," and feel the poverty state, your consciousness attracts poverty so the poor get poorer and the rich get richer.

--------~~~--------

When you try to will something into being by mental coercion or will power, you are using the law of reverse action, because it is as though you are saying, "I will be well, I will be strong, I will be wealthy," when actually what you are saying is, "I AM sick, I AM weak, I AM poor." . . Let the weak say, I AM strong.

Your subconscious is like a recording machine, and it records what you decree. Greater love hath no man than this, that a man lay down his life for his friends. Your friend is that which befriends you; therefore, you give up the old state and focus your attention on your ideal, thereby giving life to it. By getting into the mood and tonal quality and living in the reality of it, you will die to the old state and live to the new.

You must realize that the idea you have in your mind is real. It is a psychological fact. But to make it concrete or tangible, or make it appear in my world, I must sense it or get into the mood which is creative, and then walk in the light and realization that it will come to pass.

If your attitude of mind is: "Well, I might get it. I'll try, but I know it is impossible. Maybe some future time," these are moods or feelings and they will be expressed inevitably as disappointments, frustration and unrealized hopes. . This day is this scripture fulfilled in your ears.

Remember, all of us are between two thieves . . the past and the future. Nothing is accomplished by looking at either one. Many dwell on old hurts, peeves, grudges and losses of years ago. Others are full of fear regarding the future. They are afraid of old age, sickness, insecurity and death. All the good

The Power of "I AM"

you seek is now, for God is the Eternal Now! All the
attributes, qualities and potencies of God are instantly
available to you. The Spirit within you is timeless, spaceless
and ageless.

The End

Quotes resources

All the quotes in The Power of I AM are credited
to the following authors.

Neville Goddard, Joseph Murphy, Walter C. Lanyon, Walter
Devoe, Lillian DeWaters, Emmet Fox, Ella Wheeler, Christian
D Larson, Edna Lister, Thomas Troward

Books by David Allen

The Power of I AM 1, 2 and 3

The Neville Goddard Collection (All 10 of his books plus 2
Lecture series)

Neville Goddard - Your Inner Conversations are Creating
Your World

The Definitive Christian D. Larson Collection (6 Volumes, 30
books)

Neville Goddard's Interpretation of Scripture, Unlocking The
Secrets of The Bible

Neville Goddard - Imagining Creates Reality - 365 Mystical Daily
Quotes

David Allen - The Money Bible - The Secrets of Attracting
Prosperity

David Allen - The Creative Power of Thought, Man's Greatest
Discovery

David Allen - The Secrets, Mysteries & Powers of The
Subconscious Mind

www.ingramcontent.com/pod-product-compliance
Lightning Source LLC
Chambersburg PA
CBHW021827090426
42811CB00032B/2054/J